KU-760-253

Contents

Transport Policy:
The Myth of Integrated Planning

John Hibbs

Published by the Institute of Economic Affairs
2000

First published in November 2000 by
The Institute of Economic Affairs
2 Lord North Street
Westminster
London SW1P 3LB

© The Institute of Economic Affairs 2000

Hobart Paper 140
ISBN 0-255 36493-8

Many IEA publications are translated into
languages other than English or are reprinted.
Permission to translate or to reprint should
be sought from the General Director at the
address above.

Printed in Great Britain by
Hartington Fine Arts Limited, Lancing,
West Sussex
Set in Baskerville Roman 11 on 13 point

TABLES

BOXES

FOREWORD

The failures of central planning were, in the 1990s, revealed for all to see. The problems of principle inherent in planning, exposed by Hayek and others for fifty years and more, were translated into such serious problems of practice that most centrally planned regimes collapsed. Many countries which had indulged in lesser forms of planning – for example, incomes policies and 'indicative' planning – also had second thoughts. Indeed, there was such a widespread reaction against government intervention that it was claimed that 'everyone believes in markets now'.

The exaggeration implicit in that claim will be clear to readers of John Hibbs' Hobart Paper 140. The conversion to a belief in the efficacy of market forces means little if it is qualified by the view, stemming from 'Nirvana economics'[1], that there are 'imperfections' and 'failures' in most markets which justify government action. Transport is one field (though by no means the only one) which, it is argued, is different and too important to be left to the market. In particular, transport markets will, it is said, fail to provide the correct amount of co-ordination and integration. Hence arises the belief that a 'transport policy' is required: the slogan in the title of the present government's White Paper on the subject – 'integrated transport' – follows naturally.

Professor Hibbs, the author of three earlier Hobart Papers on transport, has consistently maintained that, in transport as elsewhere, the principal means by which co-ordination and integration can be achieved is through letting market forces work. As he shows in this latest Paper, the lesson has still not been learned. Governments still try

---

[1] Harold Demsetz, *Information and Efficiency: Another Viewpoint*, Journal of Law and Economics, 12(1), 1969.

to intervene, using the 'public interest' as an excuse. Indeed, in Hibbs' view, the present government's 'confused and confusing' policies towards transport '. . . promise to carry the art of meddling to new heights' (page 110). It is not only central government which is too interventionist: local authorities are again trying to re-assert control over local bus services.

The central issue identified by Professor Hibbs is that, despite all the declarations by politicians about the advantages of letting markets work, in transport they are evidently not willing to permit a price system to function. In its absence, a co-ordinated and integrated transport system is not feasible. After the privatisation of the railways, there is a form of infrastructure pricing for rail but road use is not priced. Instead, there is a crude and ineffective regime of road fuel duties (which is now leading to serious protests) and flat rate taxes on road vehicle ownership. In Hibbs' words,

> '.the greatest problem is the distortion which follows inevitably from the irrationality of infrastructure pricing.' (page 111)

There may be a need for some safety regulation and the competition authorities should keep an eye open for possible cartelisation tendencies, but otherwise Professor Hibbs wants to see an industry set free from political and bureaucratic interference.

The views in this Hobart Paper are his, not those of the Institute (which has no corporate view), its Managing Trustees, Advisers or Directors. They are intended to provoke discussion of policy in an area which appears to be one of the last refuges of central planning.

October 2000   COLIN ROBINSON
Editorial Director, Institute of Economic Affairs
Professor of Economics, University of Surrey

THE AUTHOR

JOHN HIBBS is Emeritus Professor of Transport Management at the University of Central England in Birmingham. After a managerial career in road and rail transport he moved to the academic world in 1969, but he considers himself still to be more of a practitioner than an 'academic'. As well as three *Hobart Papers* (referred to in the text) his publications include *The History of British Bus Services* (1968, 2nd edn., 1989), *The Country Bus* (1986), numerous articles in the Journals, and several textbooks on transport management and marketing. He is a Fellow of the Chartered Institute of Transport, a Member of the Institute of Transport Administration, and an Associate of the Confederation of Passenger Transport UK. Of a radical turn of mind, he has challenged the conventional wisdom in his field of study consistently throughout his career.

PREFACE

The twin themes of this paper stem from the work of two outstanding figures in the field of transport policy in the past half-century; Reuben Smeed and Gilbert Ponsonby. Smeed and his team in 1964 enunciated the case for point-of-use road pricing, which, taken forward more recently by Professor Newbery[1], leads to the conclusion that the only rigorous meaning of the term *integration* lies in the development of a rational pricing system for roads *and* 'rail roads'. Were this to be achieved, then Ponsonby's case, made in 1969[2], for co-ordination through competition, would come into its own. The words integration and co-ordination are commonly used with no real meaning, and this is one of the reasons why transport policy has been confused, and confusing, since the 1920s (if not before). I have sought here to apply them as a template, to criticise and assess the policies being developed by the present government.

For reasons of space I have limited my commentary to inland transport (including for the purpose the importance of *coastwise* shipping). For the same reason I have paid but little attention to the implications of policies emanating from the European Commission, despite Mr Kinnock's emphasis upon the development of TENS (the Trans-European Networks).

I owe a greater debt than can ever be repaid to those who have encouraged and contributed to my study of transport since 1952, most of all when I have met strong criticism

---

[1] David M. Newbery, Fair and efficient pricing and the finance of roads, *Proceedings of the Chartered Institute of Transport*, 7(3), October 1998, pp. 3–19.

[2] G. J. Ponsonby, *Transport Policy: Co-ordination through Competition*. London: IEA, Hobart Paper 49, 1969.

from the conventional wisdom of the day. For a time, I felt somewhat uncomfortable that my radical critique of bus regulation, arrived at first in 1954, had by the 1980s become something like the conventional wisdom. However, issues which had seemed plain to Mr. Ridley (as he then was) have again become confused: it seems that a policy of re-regulation and central control is now being reintroduced by the back door.

In preparing this paper I have had still more such support, along with invaluable comments and criticisms, especially from two anonymous referees – despite which, errors of fact and mistakes of judgement remain, as always, my own responsibility. Beyond and above this, my gratitude must be warmly expressed to my wife and family, for putting up with a writer in the household.

I. Introduction

The Effective and Efficient Provision of Transport: State-controlled or Market-led?

The government's *New Deal for Transport* – the 1998 White Paper – carries the slogan 'integrated transport', and assumes throughout that it is the job of government to achieve this, whatever it might mean. But neither the White Paper nor its progeny, the 'daughter documents', attempt to define the word, so perhaps a different approach to the subject is justified. Perhaps the market has a part to play in achieving integration, redefined so as to make sense of the word. Perhaps governments may not be very good at it, any way.

The subject has been my concern since my postgraduate years, when the current 'in word' was co-ordination. Since the first half of my career was in transport management, I approach it as a practitioner as well as an academic, and as one trained in sociology as well as economics. As an economist, the first of my concerns is that there should be a framework such as will tend to the efficient allocation of scarce resources. This will seem obvious, but it is rare for the subject to be discussed other than in the pages of the textbooks and the learned periodicals. There seems to be a widely held opinion that transport is in some way insulated from the normal constraints of the economic process. As a result, many people who ought to know better speak and write as if they were enthusiasts. Nevertheless, with my neo-Austrian background I am persuaded that there is no *theoretically perfect end-state* toward which the industry can be directed, and thus it is not a suitable case for planning. The future is all unknown.

However, as a sociologist my concern must be for the *effective* provision of transport services – those that the consumer wants (and, the economist within reminds me, is willing to pay for). It makes no difference whether the consumer is a passenger or a freight forwarder; the requirement is for the benefits of technical and managerial progress to be passed on with a minimum of delay (an objective not always shared by financiers, managers, bureaucrats or councillors).

Clearly there is some conflict between these two concerns, at least in the short run. The two processes do not necessarily proceed hand in hand. And it is the short run that matters to consumers, and, be it said, to politicians. Although the free market undoubtedly tends to promote efficiency, imperfections inhibit effectiveness, as has been only too often apparent in the past. The most serious of these is the misuse of regulation.

Here is the nub of the problem. For what is Mr Prescott's concept of integration but a call for more intervention, leading to the weakening of both effectiveness and efficiency? Ever since the steam railway was introduced governments have intervened in the transport industry, and today it is more regulated than at any time in its history. Yet there is a widespread assumption that transport is in some way suited to a top-down, highly subsidised regime, such as we had from 1968 to 1986, in the bus industry, until we found we could not afford it.

Planning-led solutions weaken the economy and not only constrain efficiency (which, as an economist, I would deplore), but also inhibit effectiveness (which, as a sociologist, is a quality I desire to maximise). The conclusion is plain. Within such constraints as may be needed to deal with genuine imperfections (principally safety, and issues of scale and power), because only in the market does there exist a *good, selfish reason* for managers in the industry to 'get it right', transport, including the use of cars, must be a market-based, customer-driven activity. Which is not what Mr Prescott means by integration.

This paper criticises the present government's policies as leaning still too far to central intervention and constraints on the market process, which can promote neither efficiency nor effectiveness. It challenges the widespread assumption that transport is, in some way, insulated from the principles that govern the economy at large. That is an assumption expressed recently by the President of the International Union of Public Transport (UITP), when he remarked that political authorities need to know that public transport is not 'a commercial service like all the others'.[3]. That way lies grave misallocation of resources and declining effectiveness of supply.

---

[3] Quoted in *Bus and Coach Professional*, No. 15, 1999.

II. The Government's Policy

An Invitation to Contribute

White Papers have gone trendy in recent years – all bright covers and pictures, far from the former Whitehall image of nineteenth century seriousness. The title of this one made the message plain:

A NEW DEAL FOR TRANSPORT:
BETTER FOR EVERYONE
The Government's White Paper on the Future of Transport

And, down in the left-hand corner, the slogan, in logo form, *integrated transport* (lower case). It was targeted, perhaps, at the impulse buyer (but, at £16.50, perhaps not). Along with it, separate papers for Scotland and Wales, and, to follow, a series of 'daughter papers' to extend the argument, and set out in more detail what the government intended to do. Nothing in a hurry, it would seem.

But the 1998 White Paper followed from an invitation to contribute published a year sooner, with the title *Developing an integrated transport policy*. And it is to this document we must turn for some introduction to what is meant by integration.

The key lies in paragraph 10, *The transport review*. It reads as follows:

> In undertaking this review it is clear that some stark and difficult policy choices may have to be made; and that progressively and over time we may all have to come to terms with some difficult personal choices. That is part of balancing, for example, our desire for cheap, accessible transport with the need to recognise the long-term costs to the environment. So it will be important to remember the background to our review and the aims and objectives, including those of integration, sustainable mobility, safety, affordability and cost effectiveness, which we are seeking to achieve. In particular, therefore, our review will investigate ways of ensuring that transport policy plays its part in:

- promoting environmental objectives;
- promoting economic development, across all parts of the country;
- promoting greater efficiency in the use of scarce resources, including road and rail capacity;
- enhancing the vitality of town and city centres;
- meeting the needs of rural areas;
- reducing social exclusion and taking account of the basic accessibility needs of all sectors of society, including disabled people;
- ensuring a high standard of safety across all modes, and promoting a travelling environment in which personal security is not compromised; and, crucially,
- promoting greater awareness of the issues throughout society.

Here we are promised a number of highly desirable objectives which are to be 'reviewed', including 'integration, sustainable mobility, safety, affordability and cost effectiveness'. Surely there must be some confusion of thought here? Is integration to be seen as just one objective among others, and not the great, overriding policy for the industry? The paragraph goes on to suggest that it is transport that is to be 'integrated' into a series of economic and social objectives, all of them very worthy, and extremely difficult to quantify, if a measure of success is to be achieved. And indeed it is this *olla podrida* of objectives that gives the lie to any claim that the White Paper and its daughters have some unique solution to the problems of transport; by name, integration. The theme of the White Paper was not integration: it was intervention. And Mr Prescott's Transport Bill incorporates just that. But the White Paper was also very short on the outcomes of its high-minded propositions, and it was two years after the appearance of the consultation document that some ideas about the practical consequences of Mr Prescott's meditations became available, in the daughter documents. When we compare this with the pace of Mr Ridley's reforms (the White Paper, *Buses*, of 1984, followed by the Transport Act 1985, with virtually no consultation), and with the privatisation of Railways (White Paper July 1992; Consultation Document October 1992; enactment 1993), the contrast could hardly be greater. The impression is growing that Mr Prescott's reforms had to be recast, perhaps because of the scale of the changes envisaged;

perhaps because they may now seem a long way from the sweeping changes promised before the 1997 general election.

The picture is further complicated by the existence of Scottish and Welsh versions of the White Paper, because of the powers given to the Scottish Parliament and the Welsh Assembly. We hear of dreams of new railways to unite Wales. More seriously, we reflect upon the resistance to Mr Ridley's reforms in Scotland, where a far more *dirigiste* attitude to transport can be found. The Scots managed to delay bus privatisation until it was effectively forced upon them. But for the purpose of this paper, it is best to stay with the main stream of Westminster policy.

That being so, the two daughter documents most relevant are those on road pricing and on the bus and coach industry. We will examine these, and then turn to look at some of the broader structural changes proposed in the Transport Bill itself, which is now going through parliament.

Breaking the Logjam

This, the title of the daughter document on road pricing, indicates in its very wording a political short-termism, which, although paying tribute to problems of pollution, concentrates on the issue of congestion, and which is open to the accusation of merely treating symptoms. It fails to recognise the causes of the problem: that the roads are traditionally provided free at the point of use (the zero marginal price problem); and that there is no equity in the road system as an asset (see p. 29). The combination of charging, in some form yet to be defined, with a tax on workplace parking, cannot but be seen as a draconian interference with the liberty of the subject – and of the subject's motor car.

Which indeed it is, and the document fails to distinguish between road-use pricing as 'just another tax', which is how it is commonly regarded, and its purpose to provide an equitable solution to the problems that have arisen from the lack of a pricing system for a scarce commodity. In the face of public ignorance regarding such matters, the thing will inevitably be seen as a 'poll-tax on wheels', especially if it is justified simply as a congestion tax, and it is already becoming a political shuttlecock. The danger is that its benefits may now be lost for a further generation; the immediate reaction of the Conservative party to its appearance in the Gracious Speech made one fear the worst.

There are deeper issues here, to which we shall return in the next chapter, but the document is open to the serious criticism that it is anti-car. It neglects the social and cultural aspects of the problem, perhaps because it is viewed from a London-based, middle-class angle. Table 1 demonstrates the size of working-class car ownership, and it must be remembered that, when jobs are scarce, someone with a car has a better chance of finding employment than anyone dependent upon public transport. There is a snobbish, ill-conceived, holier-than-thou attitude to the car heard too often today that inhibits rational debate, and the document fails to address it.

The private car has been a great liberator for social and work-based purposes across all the social strata. It has also caused severe harm to the social inclusiveness of local communities, within the great cities as well as in the countryside. Nevertheless, at the point of use it is the perceived gain that decides the choice between car and public transport, and freedom of choice is to be defended. Exhortations to reduce car travel will always come up against its manifest benefits. But the most serious weakness relates to the powers of local authorities. There exists no meaningful relationship between local government bound-aries and the spread of urbanisation, and the confusion and ill-will that must arise when pricing starts to be enforced for no visible reason is not hard to imagine. And beyond this there is the failure of the document to address the issue of pricing for the intercity highways and motorways, which is where a great part of the problem lies, since urban areas call for network point-pricing, which is inappropriate for longer-distance road-use.

Table 1 Travel to Work by Car: Analysis by Socio-economic Group, 1991 (10% sample)

Socio-economic Group		Numbers driving to work by car (excluding passengers)
1,2	Employers and managers	244,583
3,4	Professional workers	76,459
5	Intermediate non-manual workers	198,996
6	Junior non-manual workers	224,954
Sub-total		744,992 (59.84%)
8,9,12	Manual workers (foremen, super-isors, skilled and own account)	304,426
7,10	Personal service and semi-skilled manual workers	136,684
11	Unskilled manual workers	32,542
13,14,15	Farmers and agricultural workers	10,959
16,17	Members of armed forces and inadequately described and not stated occupants	15,347
Sub-total		499,958 (40.16%)
Total		1,244,950 (100.00%)

Source: *1991 Census Report for Great Britain Part 2*,
    Stationery Office.
These figures demonstrate that the private car is no longer merely a middle-class luxury. Given the extended choice of employment that it offers, it has clearly become a working-class necessity, as the politically correct anti-car lobby needs to regognise.

From Workhorse to Thoroughbred

If the government is not to be congratulated on the daughter paper on road-use pricing, what can be said about the future of the bus (and coach) industry, not to mention the proposed development of light rapid transit (LRT)? For it is assumed that public transport will provide one alternative to private car use, when the motorist is required to pay. The really disturbing aspect of this document is the hint of *dirigisme* that pervades it, leading to the threat of imposed Quality Contracts that would be nothing less than a step towards the introduction of franchise. If Mr Prescott's pre-election promise to re-nationalise the railways failed on account of finance, his promise to re-regulate the bus industry remains alive. We shall return to the deeper issues in Chapter 4, but this threat to return to the policies that proved so disastrous between 1968 and 1986 must be recognised and resisted.

Persuading middle-class car users to transfer to public transport will not be easy, since bus services are perceived to be the form of transport of last resort. But in many places we have seen bus companies, freed from the dead hand of regulation and of local authority control, attract new custom by investment and policies designed to move the product up market. The daughter document does little to encourage marketing management of this kind, and its policies would place greater restraints upon the industry, by increasing local authority powers. It smacks of governments' fundamental desire to meddle, and of a distrust of commercial freedom, and of the small firm.

Certainly there is much that government, central and local, can do to improve the market environment for the bus industry. But this must not be allowed to stifle competition, or to tie the hands of innovative managers. The recent report of the Audit Commission, *All Aboard*, although supporting many of the government's policies for the industry, concludes (p. 78, para. 120) that 'there are very real dangers to consumers' interests, and to the public purse, if competition in the industry is stifled'.

Nevertheless, the bus will always remain something of a workhorse, and so, for most of us, will the private car, despite all the hype that goes into its promotion. Cabinet ministers may command thoroughbreds, but the best most of us can hope for is some improvement in the choice we have got. That is how the market works. The assumption to be found in the daughter document, that local government is capable of second-guessing the market, and acting as if a supplier of first resort, is highly questionable and dangerous. What it amounts to is the threat of re-regulation, by the back door.

Integration and Co-ordination: the Power of Words

The White Paper was about integration. There is much talk today about co-ordination. Both terms are ill defined. The White Paper spoke of an integrated transport *policy*; that was the substance of the Transport Act 1947. Others speak of an integrated transport *industry*, which the British Transport Commission, set up by that statute, was incapable of achieving.[4] Yet others confuse the word integration with co-ordination, meaning the clockwork precision of trains, trams and buses provided at great public expense in countries like Switzerland, but with no opportunities for entrepreneurial innovation; with heavy social cross-subsidy; and with average cost pricing. Even there, people are asking whether it is all worth it, and some countries are turning to franchise as a cheaper way of attaining the same doubtful objectives.

However, both words are commonly seen as the practice of some superior regulator, who can direct traffic to use the most desirable service in the interests of better co-ordination; a circular argument. More goods, it is said, should go by rail (or even by canal) – self-evident, until you start to work it out in practice. Today, as a consequence of dismantling British Rail and introducing a commercial environment, more freight is moving by rail, as we shall see in Chapter 7, but there is no conceivable authority that could impose this while retaining optimum allocative efficiency.

Co-ordination from above, in this sense, is unachievable, however desirable it may appear at first sight. The Road Traffic Act 1930 directed the Traffic Commissioners, as the licencing authority for bus and coach services, to consider the needs of their area as a whole, with a view to securing the co-ordination of all forms of passenger transport, including rail; in the absence of any meaningful definition, nothing came of it. Even were it possible to bring together

---

[4] Michael Bonavia, in *The Nationalisation of British Transport*, London: Macmillan, 1987, analyses the establishment and policies of the Commission, and the reasons for its failure.

all the information needed to take the myriad decisions, the non-linear characteristics of this huge and complex industry are such as to make its central planning impossible. As Parker and Stacey put it,

> Any system which attempts conscious design or planning of long-term futures will inevitably break down. Companies and economies require structures and institutions which encourage self-transformation.[5]

But regulation can only discourage this.

And that is not all. Light-touch regulation to ensure safety is one thing, but the functions of the regulator – if this mythical co-ordination is to be pursued from above – must rest in the hands of bureaucratic administrators, who must certainly be risk-averse, and who will inevitably have their own agenda. The White Paper assumes without question that the 'platonic guardians', as Deepak Lal calls them[6] can be relied on to second-guess the market, and impose regulatory solutions upon this complex industry. Lal demonstrates convincingly that this cannot be relied on. To take but one example, the autonomous Traffic Commissioners after 1931 imposed standard, mileage-based, average cost pricing on the UK bus industry, and thereby deprived management of the ability to respond to car competition, and brought about the strange suicide of the industry thirty years later. Yet they believed they were effecting the co-ordination expected of them by the Road Traffic Act 1930.

A more rigorous, if simplistic, definition of co-ordination is the matching of supply with demand; but here again there is no 'ideal end-state', towards which planning could be directed. In the title of his paper Ponsonby[7] makes the argument plain for an ongoing process, arising from the working of the market itself, and the implication is thus that

---

[5] David Parker and Ralph Stacey, *Chaos Management and Economics*, London: IEA, Hobart Paper 125, 1994, p. 93.

[6] Deepak Lal, 'Markets, Mandarins and Mathematicians', in *Against Dirigisme*, San Francisco: ICS Press, 1994.

[7] Ponsonby 1969, *op.cit.*

integration is an irrelevance. It is my argument in this paper, following Ponsonby, that top-down integration, whether of ownership or of policy, is undesirable, and, indeed, unworkable, in the sense of achieving anything worth having. In the ill-defined sense in which it is used in the White Paper and its daughter documents it is not just irrelevant but downright dangerous. And the Transport Bill contains nothing but the same confusion, attenuated at times by the convolutions of the parliamentary draughtsmen.

A Positive Approach

There is however a sense in which the term integration can be discussed, with real potential for reform. A radical analysis of the problems of transport must turn upon the infrastructure of the industry; the system of roads and railroads, of bridges, ports and information technology around and over which the movement of goods and passengers takes place. And it is here that a fundamental problem of irrationality arises, in the limited case of the relationship between rail and road transport: the provision of the road infrastructure *free at the point of use.*

It is this zero marginal price problem that gives rise to the growing pressure for electronic road-use pricing (ERP), which we have already seen to be something that the government fails to understand, in principle. But any introduction of ERP is open to the criticism that it is merely 'treating symptoms', to use a medical analogy. The sickness lies deeper. It can be appreciated best by reminding ourselves that *nobody owns the roads.* Indeed, the definition of the highway in law is quite simply 'a path over which all members of the public have liberty to pass and repass for business or pleasure'.[8] In this situation, the ownership of the soil is irrelevant; frontagers probably own the land up to the middle of the road, but there is nothing they can do

---

[8] David M. Walker, *The Oxford Companion to Law*, Oxford: OUP, 1980, p. 570; it may appear doubtful from this whether it is permissible to park vehicles on the highway.

with it, short of agreeing to club together and charge users, and ownership conveys no responsibilities for it. Many trunk roads and all motorways have been built on land purchased by government authorities, and the same thing applies in many cases where roads have been widened or improved, but the value of such expenditure does not yet appear on any balance sheet.

The heart of the problem thus lies in the lack of any equity in the roads themselves, unlike the situation in which the railway lines are owned by Railtrack plc (see p. 29). Professor Newbery has suggested that road assets should be transferred to 'a new company, which we may call Roadtrack by analogy with Railtrack'.[9] It 'would be regulated by the 'Office of Road Regulation' (OFROAD?) which would set standards and monitor performance'.

Taking this idea further, we may consider such a corporation as being responsible for the maintenance of existing assets; for improvements and for new investment, using cash flows from users, by pricing and other means; with freedom to borrow where a measurable return on capital could be discerned; but free from the pressure that arises today from road users who see road track as a free good. The slogan, *The roads are yours: use them*, commonly found in motor car promotion in the 1930s, would no longer carry the same meaning.

Such a corporation would use electronic charging systems as one of its pricing tools. But in an open economy, goods and passengers will move over whatever form of infrastructure appears most economical. For too long the choice between road and railway has been vastly distorted by the inclusion of track costs in rail pricing, on the one hand, and not for using the roads, on the other. The *logistics* of the movement industries therefore cannot tend to optimal allocation of the scarce resources of land and capital that are involved. So why not have a single 'track authority', and have it in the private sector?

---

[9] Newbery 1998, *op. cit.*

Admittedly, Railtrack plc has been open to criticism for the way it has managed its assets, but that can be put right. A regulator (perhaps OFTRACK?) would have oversight, and the situation would be similar to that for electricity and gas, where similar 'networks' (the grids) are to be found. The case for new construction, whether rail or road, would be first of all a financial matter, so that environmental aspects could be discussed in a more objective manner than they are today. After all, environmental constraints apply to railway building as well as to new highways, and 'not in my back yard' (NIMBY) objections some years ago killed off, for the time being, a promising new freight railway through the English Midlands (see p. 62).

Whatever *integration* may or may not mean in the White Paper, the clear message is that it is to be imposed from the top. Here is the alternative: a more rigorous definition, and a proposal that the place for integration is at the bottom. Only if the funding and pricing of the infrastructure can be rationalised in this way is there any hope that Ponsonby's 'co-ordination through competition' can have a fair chance of working out. If radical reform is to mean anything for the transport industry, this is where it must begin.

Re-inventing British Rail

The performance of the railways since privatisation has been less than completely successful. We shall look at the reasons for this in more detail in Chapter 5 which discusses the future of the railways. But the Strategic Rail Authority reverts to a system that had lost credibility well before the hasty 1993 privatisation statute was introduced.

The Transport Bill suffers from a widespread misconception, which bedevilled transport policy throughout the twentieth century, of assuming that transport, and the railways in particular, are in some way 'different'. This might be called the 'railways are a national asset' philosophy, since neither road haulage nor the private car is seen in quite the same way as was British Rail (although maybe Imperial Airways was seen like this in the 1930s).

Perhaps the most interesting example of this phenomenon has been the turnabout of the media, where journalists who made British Rail their target for abuse over the years have suddenly changed their minds and called for the great days of the past!

The Strategic Rail Authority has something of that flavour. Mr Prescott is said to have observed that railways would once more be 'at the heart of our integrated transport system', but why should a mode of transport that carries 6% of the nation's passengers, and 7% of its goods, be given so great a priority in the minds of the public and their representatives? Here, surely, is the concept of integration in its most misleading and dangerous form.

The British Railways Board was never able to manage the railways, since they were the plaything of successive governments. The idea behind privatisation was to give railway companies freedom to take strategic decisions in the way that any private sector business does. The weaknesses of the new set-up – not least the financial relationship between the train operating companies and Railtrack – have become plain, and they demand reform. But, in the sacred name of integration, the Bill proposes to put the clock back.

The pseudo-British Rail that is proposed will be faced with all the problems of a nationalised industry, including the dead hand of HM Treasury, but without even the direct lines of control which the British Railways Board found so difficult to handle. With outright re-nationalisation impossible, we are to have a hybrid organisation, with minimalised freedom for directors and managers to take either strategic or tactical decisions; just as it was under British Rail. Instead of returning the railways to the full discipline of the market, we have a hybrid system with the Strategic Rail Authority, the Rail Regulator, and, in the background, the Commission for Integrated Transport all empowered to interfere in the working of the market process.

Mr Prescott's Chimera

Far from a coherent transport policy, there is a mistaken attempt to harness the private sector within a state-regulated system of franchise.

This will not work. What has appeared in the confusion of policy and politics is a strange, almost mythical beast. Perhaps unknowingly, like the sorcerer's apprentice, Mr Prescott has presented us with a chimera: a being whose head, body and tail, each having a different origin, makes up a 'grotesque monster; a thing of hybrid character; a fanciful conception', to give the dictionary definition. Mythical it may have been, but we have something very like that monster before us, and we need to take care to limit its danger.

Summing Up

Little notice is being taken in transport provision of the effective demand of the consumer, and even less of the necessity of designing a framework (in so far as this is required) that will tend to greater allocative efficiency. The present mish-mash of *dirigiste* ideas and political meddling is likely to work in the opposite direction under both of these heads. The government should consider a radical approach, integrating road and rail track pricing.

III. A Market for Road Space

The Argument for Road-use Pricing

As explained in Chapter 2 above, the problem of the roads, at heart, is that they have no equity value. When the railways were built the investment in land and the infrastructure ('track, terminals and signalling', in railway parlance) was substantial, and there is still a considerable opportunity cost involved in Railtrack's property portfolio. The infrastructure, too, neglected as it was under state ownership, has costs that must be passed on to the users. Looking to the future, investment requirements are substantial, whether for faster trains or for entirely new routes, with always the maintenance of the existing assets.

Contrast this with road transport. Here there was never any provision of equity capital, and the value of the roads as a supposed 'national asset' is impossible to measure. Replacement costs are therefore assimilated into maintenance, whereas the return on new investment is calculated on social cost/benefit terms, which are, to say the least, open to manipulation. But then, since there is no 'ownership' of the roads, in any meaningful financial sense, there can be no way to calculate what would be a satisfactory rate of return. Significantly, a cost/benefit analysis of the M1 motorway was carried out after it had been half-completed.

And there remains the problem of payment. The unit cost of railway infrastructure is measurable, even though it has been argued about ever since serious traffic costing began in the 1950s. Problems of joint cost, and of allocation to user by type of train, have been recognised and solutions have been sought. No such analysis can be meaningful for the roads, because use of the infrastructure has a zero marginal price, and therefore that no revenue arises directly from the user. Almost all expenditure on the road transport infrastructure is authorised by HM Treasury in accordance with its macro-economic policy objectives, so that the allocative benefits of private sector investment decisions and market pricing are lost. The effect of relative scarcities and the relationship between price and quality play no part in the buy/not-buy decisions of consumers, even before the problem of perceived cost[10] comes into play. Journeys that might be 'cheaper' by train or bus, or perhaps not worth making at all, given the alternative of the internet, are made without recognition of the actual costs involved, leave alone any externalities. This problem applies also where consignments of goods are concerned, and the inescapable outcome is road congestion, with all the waste and pollution that this implies.

The Politics of Road Pricing

When we analyse the issues in these terms we see the irrelevance of treating electronic road-use pricing (ERP) as nothing more than an anti-congestant; a matter of treating symptoms.[11] Only an autonomous funding agency, dependent on the market for revenue, could finance the road infrastructure so as to introduce a more rational use of the scarce resources involved. No government authority could achieve this, however stout its ring-fence. ERP would then be one of the ways by which a road track authority would raise the revenue it would need to manage its business. Its function would be comparable with the funding of railway track, and the logical development would be to combine the two businesses, as a single undertaking in the private sector

---

[10] Car users generally perceive their costs to be lower than they really are, treating most of them (including depreciation) as fixed. This is not entirely irrational, since once an asset such as a car has been acquired it is sensible to maximise its utility. But they also tend to perceive bus fares as higher than they really are, and to denigrate the quality of service. It is of course true that labour costs are virtually negligible for the car user, a problem to which we shall return in Chapter 6.

[11] See I. Heggie and P. Vickers, *Commercial Management and Financing of Roads*, World Bank Technical Paper 409, 1998.

– perhaps subject to an RPI-X cap. The managing of roads, like that of railways, must be seen to be just another economic activity, not as something felt to be unsuitable for commercial provision.

So long as congestion remains a political issue, we shall not see a development of this kind, and there is a real danger, illustrated by recent policy arguments from the Conservative party, that discussion will be at the level of perceiving ERP as 'just another tax'. It must be for those who see the underlying issues plainly to demonstrate that it is in fact the fairest way of tackling the problem, as we shall see when we examine the arguments against it. Road pricing should never be seem as a means to penalise the motorist; it is a radical solution to so many of the problems that the government's transport policy fails to address. As Professor Alan Day puts it,

> the basic economic argument for using the price mechanism wherever possible, in order to co- ordinate the decisions and actions of millions of individuals, is that it provides a flexible and subtle information system, on the basis of which the myriad decisions are made.[12]

This is a message that the politicians, together with most of the environmentalists, seem to be unable to apply to the use of the roads.

First, though, it must be emphasised that the techniques for ERP are well enough developed, and already in use, for it to be introduced, despite the pretensions of some politicians hesitant of progress for reasons related to the vote motive.[13] The 'decremental smart card', which charges the user when space is in short supply, and gives an aural and/or visual indication, is ideal for the car user. An introductory period during which the system was working but with no charge would enable users to plan alternatives for use when pricing began. No doubt road freight

---

[12] Alan Day, The case for road pricing, *Economic Affairs*, 18(4), December 1998, p. 5.

[13] See Gordon Tullock, *The Vote Motive*, London: IEA, Hobart Paperback 9, 1976.

businesses would pass the costs on to their customers (depending on the elasticity of demand). But any increase in commodity prices that would follow would simply internalise some of the unallocated costs that give rise to the problem. Operators of regular bus and coach services could commute the payments on a mileage basis, whereas the coaching trade would be in the same position as the freight operators. Fire engines and ambulances should be exempt, but not doctors, police cars on routine duties, or any kind of government vehicle. Not even the Lord Mayor – or the new Mayor of London.

But politics is about the trading-off of interests, and it is reasonable to look for a *quid pro quo* that would make pricing for scarce road space more acceptable. The Vehicle Excise Duty (VED) is a convenient example. It bears inequitably on car users, irrespective of their annual mileage, and it is an indefensible burden on people living in rural areas, for whom public transport can never be an effective alternative to the car. Like the fuel duty (which would undoubtedly continue), VED is a form of sumptuary taxation, and it were best for this to be recognised by the car-owning public. In its application to commercial vehicles it is an unjustified burden, not least in its function as a barrier to entry. It should be swept away, as part of a trade-off to make road pricing acceptable: if a more sweeping reform, such as has been suggested by Peter Mumford[14] were to be introduced, then the fuel duty could go too.

It is generally accepted that revenue from road-use pricing should be ring-fenced, but the really important political issue is to determine what is to be done with such revenue – which would amount to a considerable sum. And it is here that the importance of an autonomous authority must be stressed, free from government direction in its policies. The function of OFROAD (if so it be) must be limited to the management and improvement of the

---

[14] Peter Mumford, *The Road from Inequity; Fairer ways of paying for the true costs of road use*. London: Adam Smith Institute, 2000.

infrastructure, and the design and funding of new investment, and on no account must ERP revenue be used for subsidy to public transport operators, which would bring council bureaucrats back into management and put an end to much valuable innovation. Investment in bus priority schemes, such as sections of kerb-guided bus route, would be justified in the short run, to improve the alternative to car use. This may be seen as a proper duty of any road authority. But light rapid transit, with its heavy investment in new vehicles, power supply and premises, as well as its dedicated infrastructure, should not be funded from this source (see Chapter 5).

One final point. Some commentators regard road-use pricing as a form of *tolling*, for entry to towns or sectors of cities; others see it as *point-pricing*, applying a charge on any section of road where there is congestion. The difference between the two is important; point-pricing can be relied upon to constrain the use of cars, whereas tolling could lead an authority to encourage car use, in order to increase revenue.

Objections to Electronic Road-use Pricing

Apart from the accusation that ERP would be a 'poll-tax on wheels', there are various objections to its introduction which must now be examined. We have already seen that 'the freedom of the roads' is irrelevant, because of the fundamental need for them to be seen as a commercial undertaking. In the same way we have seen that ERP must be recognised for what it is: a *price mechanism* for dealing with problems of scarcity, which must not be labelled as *just another tax*. The remaining objections may be expressed as a series of slogans.

- *It's unfair on the poor.* There is an understandable image of the 'fat cat' driving along without bothering about the charge, but in practice people tend to watch their expenditure, so that they would be able to use priced sections of road when it was in their interest to do so, and find alternatives at other places and times. The less well-off, who are increasingly likely to own cars (see Table 1), will be in the same position, and they too will choose to pay when it suits them to do so. This, after all, is how the market for foodstuffs works, and no-one suggests that it is unfair for some to seek value for money at Waitrose and others at ALDI. In any case, one outcome of ERP would be greatly improved bus and coach services, whereas today's congestion makes for poor and unreliable services in the areas where they tend to be most used; for the quarter of households without a car this would produce a positive and recognisable gain.

- *Help, it's Big Brother!* One of the earliest examples of road-use pricing failed to attract support because it was based on the recognition of car number-plates, with a bill sent at the end of the quarter. Any such system must run up against the fear that your position at any particular time would be on record, and that one might not want one's employer, or partner, to find out. This is the 'civil liberties' argument, though it has slipped considerably since today's television cameras follow us on the streets of every town. That does not make it entirely irrelevant, but there is a powerful reason why it is unlikely to arise. Any system that depends on subsequent payment can be likened to the telephone bill – we complain when we have to pay it, but it has little rationing effect upon our use of the phone. That is why, from the first, proponents of ERP have advocated what we know today as decremental smart cards, so that the driver *knows* when a charge is being made.

- *But I'm a doctor!* Claims for special treatment, whether by doctors, cabinet ministers, lord mayors or chief constables, fail the equity test that is essential if ERP is to be politically acceptable. Emergency vehicles – fire, ambulance and coastguard services – are worthy of exemption, but if it were to apply to all police vehicles at all times the system would be at risk of falling into disrepute. OFROAD must be a commercial organisation, and not an adjudicator of other priorities.

- *They'll all come past my gate.* Many fear that ERP would lead to road users finding alternative routes that were not priced. For urban purposes the answer must be to have a multiplicity of pricing points, so that congestion is charged wherever it emerges (which includes congestion at out-of-town shopping centres). There is still the danger of 'rat-running', but residential streets (other than cul-de-sacs) need only have a charging point at one end to deter the rat-runner, while permitting residents to avoid it. The problem is more serious where the inter-urban highway system is concerned, since motorway pricing would certainly lead to greater use of other roads. For this purpose ERP would have to apply to the whole system, with suitable provision for the prevention of rat-running, and traffic management schemes where appropriate.

Each of these objections, and others as well, deserve to be heard. The man or woman on the Clapham omnibus should never be disdained as a critic of public policy. Even if misinformed, such criticism influences public opinion, and is reflected in the media. The best answer is to stress the essentially equitable nature of ERP. Ultimately the problem lies in the inescapable scarcity of land and the multiplicity of uses to which it can be put. Mark Twain is reported to have said: 'When they ask me what to put their money in, I tell 'em, land. I have it on the highest authority they ain't makin' any more'. The introduction of effective road-use pricing (*not tolling*), to replace the present method of payment, which is 'zero at the point of sale', must lie at the heart of any transport policy aimed to integrate car and public transport – market-led.[15]

Summing Up

No one can defend the existing system for providing roads. It is inequitable, ineffective, and inefficient in the allocation of the scarce resources involved. Ever suspicious of radical reform, the British could all too easily be sold the idea of ERP as no more than a means of dealing with congestion; even worse, the politically correct may see it as another means of harassing the motorist. The heart of the argument for it must always be the gain in allocative efficiency.

---

[15] The subject has been discussed at greater length in *Economic Affairs*, 18(4), December 1998, with articles by Alan Day, Gabriel Roth, Paul Truelove, Stephen Ison, David Bayliss, Peter Hills and the present author.

IV. Franchise – the Mirage

Neither Effective nor Efficient

The benefits of privatisation have been recognised widely during the past two decades, and not least in the case of transport services. In the United Kingdom the process began with the disposal of a large part of the state-owned lorry fleet after 1953, carried further by the privatisation of the National Freight Corporation, under a Labour government, in 1969. After taking power in 1979 the Conservatives paid more attention to deregulation, and indeed it would seem that the privatisation of the bus industry was something of an afterthought in the drafting of the Transport Act 1985.[16] Even then the idea of privatising the railways was unthinkable in the higher reaches of government at the time.

The Transport Act 1968, often associated with the name of Barbara Castle, was designed to give powers to local government to supervise the bus industry, and in effect municipalised the state-owned bus companies in what were to become the metropolitan counties. All bus operators, and British Rail, were required to co-operate with each other and with the local authority, and powers of 'co-ordination' were given to county councils in England and Wales, with similar intervention in Scotland. The Act also provided for subsidy, which was expected to help to solve the 'rural transport problem'.

---

[16] Dr Matthew Bradley and I concluded that the proponents of bus deregulation, of whom I was one, failed to pay sufficient attention to the process and timing of privatisation, as to which little had been written in 1984. It thereafter became a messy and politicised development, so that the benefits of deregulation itself were unduly delayed. See John Hibbs and Matthew Bradley, *Deregulated Decade: ten years of bus deregulation*, London: Adam Smith Institute, 1997.

One effect of this was to make bus managers the agents of local authority planners, with predictable consequences in terms of public choice and the vote motive. In the early 1980s managers were complaining to me that officials and councillors were requiring them to pay so much attention to minor service adjustments that they were unable to develop the main revenue-earning routes. With their powers of subsidy the 'co-ordinators' were able to impose their own policies on the operators, and while many of their decisions were politically motivated, only too few were market-driven. The bureaucrat, after all, quite properly should be risk-averse.

The volume of subsidy, which rose from £117 million in 1978/79 to some £400 million in 1984/85, frightened HM Treasury (which may account for parliamentary time being found for the Transport Act 1985), but the fact that 80 per cent of it was being directed to London and the metropolitan counties, which were the easiest areas in which to operate profitably, came as a surprise. Furthermore, as Table 2 shows, this expenditure failed to stem the loss of traffic from public transport.

Who Is to Run Public Transport?

The state-owned (and highly bureaucratic) National Bus Company (NBC), which in 1984 owned roughly one third of the bus and coach fleet in England and Wales, turned out to have nurtured a remarkable set of young and entrepreneurial managers. Whereas in Ireland, north and south, bus services have for long been very largely the responsibility of a single parastatal undertaking, the NBC had retained a holding company structure, so that it was possible for the individual subsidiaries to be sold off. The process commenced before deregulation was complete, and before long most of the early management or staff and management buy-outs had been acquired by the group of

**Table 2 Bus Passenger Journeys Lost under Different
Organisational Structures**

Period	Passenger miles lost (millions)	Average loss per year (millions)	Average annual rate of decline (%)
1 1950–1970[a]	7,758	387.9	-3.5
2 1970-1974[b]	971	242.8	-3.0
3 1974-1985/86[c]	2,075	188.6	-3.2
4 1985/6-1990/91[d]	1,304	116.9	-2.2
5 1991/2-1997/8[e]	328	54.6	-1.2

[a] 'Regulated monopoly' under the Road Traffic Act 1930.

[b] Following the introduction of the provisions of the Transport Act 1968 and the formation of the National Bus Company, the Scottish Bus Group and the Passenger Transport Executives. Two thirds of the industry is now in public ownership.

[c] Following the introduction of the Local Government Act 1972, with the identification of the new Metropolitan County Councils as Passenger Transport Authorities, and the development of network subsidy.

[d] The period immediately following deregulation and privatisation.

[e] The decline slows as privatisation and other benefits work their way through after the immediate upheaval which in some areas followed deregulation. Over the last four years the slow down in the rate of decline has been even more marked, and the movement either way has been less than 1%. In certain areas there has been a distinguishable upturn in bus carryings, a significant part of it representing a shift from travel by car.

Source: Bus Industry Monitor 1999, courtesy of
TAS Publications & Events.

holding companies that exist today.[17] The 1985 Act required the municipal undertakings, and those of the metropolitan county councils, to be set up as joint-stock

---

[17] The OFT insisted on a 'patchwork quilt' pattern of acquisition, so that territorial dominance is limited, and, individual acquisitions apart, further concentration of ownership is unlikely to be allowed.

companies, with a view to privatisation, and today all but 17 of them have been acquired by the major groups.[18] In the metropolitan counties, however, where subsidy was concentrated, highly political issues were involved, and resistance to privatisation was very strong. A side-effect of this was the mishandling of deregulation in certain cases, most notably Greater Manchester (see p.69), which attracted criticism disproportionate to the generally beneficial results of the policy. Full commercial independence was thus late in reaching certain areas, but entrepreneurial management is now fairly general in bus companies throughout Great Britain; although there are some exceptions to that statement, as comment in the trade press from time to time points out.

In the former metropolitan counties the Passenger Transport Authorities, directing the policy of their Passenger Transport Executives, were in the business of running buses; indeed, while the county councils remained they were in effect the municipal transport committee. In the shire counties the extent of control varied considerably, some of them taking little action, whereas others required buses on subsidised services to carry the council's livery. The effect of the Transport Act 1985 was to drastically curtail the powers of the various authorities, and this was widely resented. Their residual power to intervene in the market lies in the use of subsidy by tender for the provision of 'socially necessary' services; extended recently when the present government decided, as we shall see (p. 91) to throw money at the rural transport problem.

The Return of *Dirigisme*

An initial reaction to the loss of the authorities' planning powers was to seek to have little to do with the newly commercialised bus industry. Highway authorities in par-

---

[18] An interesting defence of the 'municipal company' has been put forward – see Barry J. C. Moore, The Municipal Bus Company – an Appropriate Ownership, *Proceedings of the Chartered Institute of Transport* 2(3), November 1993, pp. 40–45. Mr Moore was at the time General Manager of the progressive Ipswich undertaking.

ticular had little incentive to co-operate with bus managers, and the development of pedestrianisation, for example, proceeded in many towns and cities with little or no attention being paid to its consequences for the local bus companies.[19] But the bus industry was itself open to criticism at this time, since the conurbation companies, still publicly owned, took so long to introduce effective marketing management.

Writing in 1996, Gavin Booth, a respected commentator on the bus industry, remarked

> If deregulation and privatisation had not happened, what state would the industry be in today? A pretty desperate one! The mid-1980s recession would have forced some action, and no doubt there would have been staff and vehicles sacrificed in the name of economies, but we really needed the 'fresh start' of the Stagecoaches of this world to bring new thinking to the bus industry.[20]

Others have suggested that without the 1985 reforms the industry would have declined to the extent that it has in many US cities, where public transit hardly exists at all.

This may indeed be true, but in the interim the planners discovered that many continental cities had retained and developed the electric tramway, and light rapid transit (LRT) was invented as a means to restore direct operating powers. After the special case of Manchester, which is not an example of 'pure' LRT, experience of the Sheffield Supertram (see p. 83) led HM Treasury to distrust investment of this kind, which we shall criticise further in Chapter 6. Local authority councillors and planners then, especially in the Passenger Transport Authorities, jumped on the integration bandwagon, and saw the potential of franchise.

Reversing Deregulation

Exploiting the efficiencies of the private sector while

---

[19] There is reason to suppose that pedestrianisation actually encourages greater car use, as the buses are removed from the shopping areas, yet multistorey car parks continue to give access to the motorist.

[20] Gavin Booth, 1986 and all that, *Proceedings of the Chartered Institute of Transport* 6(2), June 1997, pp. 11–25.

maintaining control of the operations of the industry has been a policy pursued in many countries, and it has obvious attractions for the planner. It was, of course, the philosophy that produced the situation in London today.[21] Fearful, it would seem, to deregulate so close to the politicians' front door, the government in 1984 set up a system of tendering for London Transport's bus services, open to both private operators and to subsidiaries of London Buses Limited (LBL), the statutory authority. In 1994-95 the eleven LBL companies were privatised: five were management buy-outs (MBOs), and the remainder went to a number of different interests. None of the MBO companies remains independent today.

Much praised, the London system is nothing more than a device for forcing down costs, while giving managers no opportunity to exploit the market in the interests of either efficiency or effectiveness. The 'Framework Agreement', followed by the 'Route Agreement', to which the successful tenderer is committed, are typically bureaucratic documents, which bind managers hand and foot to operate as LBL requires. Yet among Mr Livingstone's earliest actions has been to impose further restrictions upon the London bus companies, among other things by imposing the additional cost of employing conductors on one-man buses. The success of deregulation (along with privatisation) outwith the London Transport Area, turns essentially on the liberty that it gave to entrepreneurs, and the enthusiasm with which that liberty was used.

This liberty is denied to the bus company managers in London, yet this is the framework that some would extend to the rest of the country, on the specious grounds that deregulation has been a disaster. Note that this regime would not reverse privatisation; it is clear that what is looked for is the control of the industry, while leaving its ownership in the more efficient private sector. The confusion of thought is then plain to see; for the efficiency

[21] Analysed in *Don't Stop The Bus – Giving bus managers the freedom to manage*, by John Hibbs: London, Adam Smith Institute, 1999.

of the private bus companies is closely linked to their dynamic *effectiveness* in finding out and satisfying demand that was unsought by the publicly owned operators for many years before 1986.[22]

The introduction of franchise would be a certain failure in terms of both efficiency and effectiveness. Public authorities are ill-equipped to second-guess the market, and are culturally committed to 'planning solutions'. Because they are responsible for public money, their administrators must be risk-averse, but, unlike managers in the market, they are unlikely to suffer any penalty for getting their decisions wrong.

That apart, the term franchise is being used here in a special sense, very far from the familiar examples for fast food, cosmetics or clothing. In such businesses the franchisee is in competition with other firms, while paying for the advantage of a trading name with a reputation for quality. Those who advocate franchise by tender for the bus industry speak of firms 'competing *for* the market' instead of competing *in* the market'.[23] This, very plainly, is an economic fallacy of the first order; what is meant is competing for a monopoly. Not at all the same thing! (The rail franchises, as we shall see in the next chapter, are somewhat different, and more of a hybrid example of the breed).

The record of the county councils and Passenger Transport Executives in the design and sponsorship of 'socially necessary' bus services, and the use of the recent Rural Bus Grant (to which we shall turn in Chapter 6, The Rural Problem), cannot give us much confidence in the way

---

[22] In the Birmingham suburb of Erdington, on D-day for deregulation, a private company started a service linking housing estates to the High Street which could have been introduced thirty years earlier by the then Birmingham City Transport. Running hourly at first, it was soon increased to half-hourly, and continues to carry good loads today. Numerous similar developments have followed, bringing the buses closer to people's homes, with no need for subsidy.

[23] The term has been around for a long time. The earliest example I have been able to find which refers to the bus industry is in Ian Savage's book, *The Deregulation of Bus Services*, London: Gower, 1985, p. 255.

they would operate through franchise. It is impossible to define what is socially necessary in any rigorous fashion, and the exigencies of public finance make the relative availability of funds a controlling factor. The outcome may vary from intervention in some part of the market process to the operation of buses carrying a great deal of fresh air at public expense. To extend these activities to a full franchise, with all decisions taken by public sector managers, would be to remove the provision of bus services from the discipline of the market entirely. Franchise, as it is proposed today, is but the mirage of a regime unattainable by this means. Among interests of both left and right there is an assumption that public transport *ought* to be provided by public authorities, and the pressure for franchise is seen as a means of attaining that control. It must be strongly resisted. However, it has been provided for in the Transport Bill, and if adopted it would undo all the good that has been achieved since 1985.

The risk, though, is more serious than perhaps most commentators realise. Speaking recently at a conference organised by the International Road Transport Union[24], Gunther Hanreich, Director of Land Transport for DG VII in the European Commission, '. . . warned that a new Europe-wide strategy on transport includes recommendations for London-style tendering across the EU'.[25]

Summing Up

The atavistic pressure from councillors and officials in the public sector and the planning profession, who would hark back to the bad days of the 1970s, when passenger services were run for the satisfaction of those responsible for them,

---

[24] Reported in the magazine *Bus and Coach Professional*, 19 October 1999.

[25] A wide-ranging paper from Brussels sets this proposition out in detail, and should be met with radical criticism by market economists concerned with the industry (*Proposal for a Regulation of the European Parliament and of the Council on action by Member States concerning public service requirements and the award of public service contracts in passenger transport by rail, road and inland waterway*. Brussels, 26.7.2000, COM(2000) 7 Provisional. 2000/0212 (COD)).

and at great public expense, must be resisted. The concept of franchise as a means of holding down costs is in no way a substitute for a market-driven industry, which tends to effective supply and the kind of efficiency that cannot be achieved by the platonic guardians. 'Re-regulation', which Mr Prescott promised in 1997, and which is potentially attainable under the Transport Bill, could return the industry to the days when managers failed to define their market, political interference was rife, and the efficient provision of services to satisfy demand had given way to wasteful expenditure and uncontrolled cross-subsidy – generally at the expense of the poor.

V. Railways Making Progress

The State of Public Knowledge

It may still be hard to convince the British electorate that transport is just another service industry, subject to the same marketing characteristics as hairdressing or accountancy, even now that much of the shift of ownership from the public to the private sector seems to be irreversible. It is seldom questioned in the case of air or road freight transport, or even the port industry, yet for buses and trains there is still a tendency to look back and see a golden age of state or municipal ownership, which certainly never existed. In this chapter we shall look at railway passenger services, recognising that they are not (and can never be) perfect, but looking to the future, to see where they can be expected to improve further.

Politicians and the public alike appear to possess certain fixed ideas about railways that are by no means related to reality.[26] A certain sentimental attraction may be their association with childhood train-sets. Anyone who experienced the floods of quite irrational emotion that accompanied the resistance to close even the least-used lines during the 1960s will be familiar with the problems we face when dealing with what Sir Christopher Foster, as long ago as 1963, called 'the transport problem'.[27] The quantity of enthusiast and nostalgic literature on railways beggars belief.

---

[26] The hysteria shown by the media following the railway disaster at Ladbroke Grove in October 1999 was out of all proportion to the scale of carnage on the streets of our towns and cities every week of the year.

[27] C. D. Foster, *The Transport Problem*, Glasgow: Blackie, 1963; 2nd, revised edn., London: Croom Helm, 1975.

State intervention is as old as the steam railway itself. Railways are fail-dangerous (see below) and the common law maxim *caveat emptor* ('let the buyer beware') cannot apply to them. Safety regulation is therefore appropriate, but parliaments from the first were suspicious of their potential monopoly, and of a tendency to combination and territorial monopoly. Following traders' complaints of discrimination, the Railway & Canal Traffic Act of 1888 introduced price control, and from then on the goal of state ownership became ever plainer. The Railways Act of 1921 restructured the industry, but parliament failed to recognise that the growth of commercial motor transport had ended the danger of monopoly, leaving the railway companies to compete with their hands tied. So by 1939 there was probably a general acceptance that nationalisation was the next step.[28]

It is therefore important to recognise that the acquisition of the companies by the newly formed British Transport Commission in 1947 was not a controversial issue in party political terms. Policy thereafter followed the twin tracks of seeking to improve the structure of the undertaking and of starving it of the funds necessary for its efficient operation. As a corporation, British Railways lacked direction, and suffered from the winds of political change. By the 1990s morale and efficiency were beginning to improve, but the influence of HM Treasury remained a damper on innovation, and the Board lacked the freedom of a public company to direct its own affairs.

By the late 1980s the logic of privatisation was being recognised within a limited circle. As early as 1984 David

---

[28] A recent article supports this, and argues that '. . . the consensual terms in which public ownership was advocated in the inter-war years did not help the nationalised railways to cope with post-war conditions and issues'. (Gerald Crompton, Good business for the nation': the railway nationalisation issue, 1921–1947, *Journal of Transport History*, 20(2), September 1999, pp. 141–159).

Starkie had written about it,[29] but although Downing Street took a keen interest in the mid-1980s, this seems to have cooled, perhaps because of the issues associated with bus privatisation. So the Railways Act 1993, which set the wheels in motion, was a late runner, facing the likely possibility that signals would change at the next general election (which of course to some extent they did, but see p. 54), and the railways continued to be a political issue as they had been since 1830. To complicate matters, the European Commission at the same time issued a Directive requiring railway administrations in the EU to make a clear distinction between the operational and infrastructure parts of the business.

The Times on 29 June 1989 reported that Downing Street had identified six options, which were as follows:[30]

- *Privatisation of British Railways as one railway and one company.* This was the preference of the British Railways Board, which argued that substantial improvements had already been made in structure and management, and that the railway was financially healthy.

- *Privatisation as a single holding company with a range of subsidiaries.* This was essentially a variant of the previous option.

- *Establishment of a track authority or company to own the infrastructure, with a range of private companies to operate the*

---

[29] David Starkie, BR – Privatisation Without Tears, in *Economic Affairs*, October–December 1984. Reprinted as 'British Railways: opportunities for a contestable market', in *Privatisation & Regulation – the UK Experience*, John Kay, Colin Mayer and David Thompson (eds), Oxford: Clarendon Press, 1986, reprinted 1989. Interestingly, the editors regarded the railways as a natural monopoly. The same article also appeared as 'British Rail: competition on the network' in Cento Veljanovski (ed.), *Privatisation and Competition: A Market Prospectus*, London: IEA, Hobart Paperback 28, 1989.

[30] See Stephen Glaister, June Burnham, Handley Stevens and Tony Travers, *Transport Policy in Britain'* London: Macmillan, 1989, p. 42. I am indebted to this book for the analysis that follows.

services. This option, which was eventually selected, was put forward by the Adam Smith Institute.[31]

- *Privatisation as separate territorial companies.* While seen by some as reverting to the 'four main lines', the companies created by statute in 1923 and nationalised in 1947, this option would have permitted the formation of a number of companies based on an analysis of their prospective viability. Such companies would have retained vertical integration of operations and infrastructure, which was advocated by some senior railway officials on efficiency grounds. Favoured by the Centre for Policy Studies, this option came to be the preferred choice of the Prime Minister, John Major.[32]

- *Privatisation on the basis of Business Sectors.* British Rail had decentralised management on this pattern, defining the InterCity network, Regional Railways, Network SouthEast, and the freight and parcels businesses, with a separate administration for the infrastructure. It produced problems of allocation of both costs (especially track costs) and of revenue, and attracted little support.

- *Retention of the status quo.* Although this was not seriously considered by government, it was undoubtedly favoured by the majority of the electorate (with their emotional commitment to the railway), as well as by not a few MPs. Despite its long-standing denigration of British Rail (and its sandwiches) the media generally regarded privatisation with considerable reserve. Paul Salveson's radical alternative did, however, present the case for a different future.[33]

In due course the preference of HM Treasury for the third option over the choice of Downing Street for the

[31] See Kenneth Irvine, *The Right Lines*, London: Adam Smith Institute, 1987; Kenneth Irvine, *Track to the Future*, London: Adam Smith Institute, 1988; and Michael Barclay, Kenneth Irvine and Anthony Shephard, *New Ideas in Train*, London: Adam Smith Institute, 1989.

[32] See Andrew Gritten, *Reviving the Railways – a Victorian Future?* London: CPC, 1988.

[33] Paul Salveson, *British Rail – the radical alternative to privatisation*, Manchester: Centre for Local Economic Strategies, 1989.

fourth option[34] won the day, and the Railways Act 1993 introduced a limited form of 'open access', which Glaister *et al.* suggest was 'strongly supported by freight customers or operators', although 'nearly all potential passenger-train operators were opposed'.[35] Mr MacGregor's White Paper, *New Opportunities for the Railways – The Privatisation of British Rail* (Cm 2012), appeared in July 1992.

The Railways Act 1993

This Act was a curious hybrid. It created a public corporation (Railtrack, later privatised as Railtrack plc) to own and manage the infrastructure, and with it a series of privately owned contractors to take care of the engineering as its agents. This at one stroke met the terms of the EC Directive 91/440, requiring the separation of railway accounts for service provision and for infrastructure, which was intended to encourage open access by way of a charging system for infrastructure use. (It will be noted that the Directive did not *require* the establishment of separate ownership regimes.) I have heard it said that HM Treasury pressed for the division of ownership, and the establishment of a corporation highly suitable for privatisation.

Railtrack was to be funded by the train operating companies, passenger and freight, through track charging, but its responsibilities for the infrastructure were to be carried out by contract with a range of privately owned Infrastructure Service Companies (initially based on the various departments of British Rail Engineering). The

---

[34] In supporting the fourth option in my own advice to the Prime Minister I added the proviso that the erstwhile Railway Clearing House be re-instated, to own and operate the ticketing system and the booking offices, redistributing revenue in accordance with mileage travelled on each company's tracks.

[35] Glaister *et al. op cit*, pp. 128–129.

Freightliner business was privatised,[36] and Railfreight was divided into three companies for privatisation, which were subsequently acquired by the Wisconsin Central Railroad, an American firm which operates them profitably and with significant expansion as English Welsh and Scottish Railways.

On the passenger side the approach was different. Instead of setting up companies for privatisation, Passenger Train Operating Units (PTOUs) were delineated,[37] whose operations were offered on the market by tender. Those who were awarded the franchises became known as Train Operating Companies (TOCs), and the management of the system was placed in the hands of the Office of Passenger Rail Franchising (OPRAF), alongside which there was placed the Rail Regulator (OFRAIL), whose responsibilities comprised:

- overseeing the arrangements for track access and charging over the whole network
- promoting competition and preventing abuse of monopoly power and anti-competitive practices
- promoting the interests of consumers and ensuring that network benefits were maintained.

Railtrack, as we have seen, is funded by access charges to the users, both passenger and freight. It has also continued the British Rail policy of disposing of surplus land. What was intended to be a decreasing proportion of this revenue originates in direct subsidy to the TOCs. But whereas the freight companies own their own rolling stock, for the TOCs this was to be leased, and the Act provided for Rolling Stock

---

[36] Freightliners are permanently coupled trains of wagons on to which standard containers are loaded, and which run fast timings on predetermined schedules. Developed in the 1960s, their efficiency was undermined when the trade unions were allowed to bar access by private hauliers to their terminals. After that they came to be limited to collection and delivery of containers for shipping lines, though it is expected that they will now return to the inland transport market for which they were intended.

[37] See *The Franchising of Passenger Rail Services – A Consultation Document*, Department of Transport, October 1992.

Companies (ROSCOs), which acquired the existing British Rail stock, and which have commissioned new construction for their clients. (The TOCs were subsequently permitted to purchase their own rolling stock.) The purpose of this is related to the franchise system within which the TOCs must work.

Each franchise must be for a specific term, and quasi-monopolistic franchises produce problems when they come up for renewal. If the TOCs owned their assets their innovative potential would be undermined by the likelihood of losing the franchise while still owning the trains. (Similar problems have been experienced with the franchises for commercial television.) The ROSCOs were thus a central element in the franchise system, which would have had no place in a fully privatised dispensation. One outcome has been the need for the Rail Regulator to limit the possibility of a ROSCO being joined with one or more TOCs by way of vertical integration.

The franchises were intended to be the key to resolving the problem of long-term under-funding of the railway. It had long been plain that HM Treasury would never be able or willing to make up for the financial neglect of the period of national ownership, and one cannot but respect the device chosen to attract private sector money to come to the rescue, while leaving the system, at the end of the day, entirely in private ownership. This was to be the magic add-on to the expectation that privatisation would improve efficiency as it had done for the bus industry.

With one exception, the Gatwick Express, each franchise carried with it a subsidy, which was to be reduced over time, and which it was to be the responsibility of the franchisee to replace, by or before the end of the period, with, in some cases, an element of repayment towards the end of the franchise. Successful tenderers, other things being equal, were those that offered the most attractive terms. Private enterprise was thus to be enticed into the railway industry at second hand, as it were, but full privatisation was postponed to the indefinite future; indeed, had not Railtrack been sold in 1997, private ownership would have been limited to the Infrastructure Service Companies and the ROSCOs. In the outcome it would appear that the Department of Transport (as it then was) had managed to retain control over the railway to an extent which questions the use of the word privatisation.

The process has a certain political fascination, not least in view of the speed with which it was pursued. There seems little doubt that we do not have the whole story, either – in July 1999 a scathing criticism in *The Economist*[38] claimed that concessionaires were attracted by substantial sweeteners paid at the expense of the public. The objective of policy might seem to have been to spike the guns of any incoming government of another party, but *The Times* suggested that 'The huge investment backlog doubtless helped to persuade Mr Blair to help John Major to sell Railtrack'.[39] What was not foreseen, however, in the haste that marked the passage of the 1993 Act, was the difference between Railtrack as a state corporation and Railtrack plc. It would appear that many of the problems that have beset the privatised railway – at a time when demand from both passenger and freight customers was growing so fast – have arisen from weaknesses in the powers of the Regulator after the sale.

Where Are They Going?

Railways are fail-dangerous. If anything goes wrong, it is difficult to escape the consequences because of the speed of the train; also, the complexity of the system is such that minor human or mechanical failure can lead to catastrophic results. The railways are, however, very safe (especially when compared with the private car or the motor-cycle), which is why the occasional accident attracts notice, whereas the multitude of fatalities on the roads does not.

The reason for this lies in something that has been called 'the culture of the rail', although it has been nurtured for

---

[38] Britain's railways: the retail billionaires, *The Economist*, 3 July 1999.

[39] *The Times*, 23 February 2000.

many years by Her Majesty's Inspectors of Railways (first established by the Railway Regulation Act 1840, and now part of the Health and Safety Executive). Fail-dangerous industries – a good example is shipping – have conservative traditions, built on the consequences of experience, which is itself good enough reason to resist change. Although the railway today is far more complex, its operating principles have remained the same since they were arrived at in the early days of steam, and even before. Until quite recently, managers were known as Railway Officers, and, although the term Railway Servant for operative staff fell into disuse after the Second World War, the concept of belonging to 'the railway service', which was to be found at all levels, has not long disappeared.

This closed world of the railway, with its inherent feeling of superiority over road transport, and its dangerous assumption that its business was running trains, rather than moving people and goods, was first threatened by Dr Beeching's necessary economy measures, resisted as they were with no little emotion by the railwaymen (they were all men) of the day. But the virtues of the tradition remained, with performance steadily improving through the latter days of British Rail, some changes in management structure notwithstanding. So the introduction of private sector management came as something of a shock, and not all of the hard-headed new managers understood or respected the culture in which they found themselves.

In due course Railtrack plc, the TOCs, and the other new creations attracted considerable new investment, and substantial savings were expected to come from cutting labour costs, as had been the case in the privatised bus companies. The short-termism that lay behind this meant that action was expected quickly. Christian Wolmar, in a generally supportive study of the career of Brian and Ann Souter,[40] makes no bones about the South West Trains experience, when former bus company managers dis-

---

[40] Christian Wolmar, *Stagecoach: A classic rags-to-riches tale from the frontiers of capitalism*, London: Orion Business Books, 1998, pp. 134 ff.

covered, the hard way, that they were in a different kind of business.

It would be wrong, though, to generalise from the high-profile mistakes that caught the attention of the media, and led to cries of 'bring back British Rail' from journalists with a very short memory. Although there are cases where the tender price was cut too close and the franchisee has problems in maintaining the requisite standards, there are remarkable examples of success. (*Stagecoach* moved quickly to deal with their South West Trains problem, and Wolmar's observation that 'by the end of 1997, only one of the original twelve senior managers Stagecoach had inherited from BR remained' is an interesting comment on the problems of conflicting culture.) However, the image of privatisation was damaged by the problems of the period – and problems were to some extent inevitable. Not surprisingly the media made the most of it, and the success stories are little-known. The growth of passenger traffic (see Table 3) has been substantial, despite the growth in the number of complaints (the latter may follow the previous reluctance to complain to British Rail), This growth is not easily accounted for, not least since fares have been increased on many services, and for some companies it has been something of an embarrassment.

What is often forgotten is the time that it takes to construct new rolling stock, to renew track and signalling, with improvements in each, and to rebuild or upgrade railway stations. Even so, effective management can do a lot to improve the service, as has been shown on the London, Tilbury & Southend, formerly known as the 'misery line'. And it has to be acknowledged that Railtrack is open to criticism in the matter of maintenance, leading to delays which are generally blamed by passengers on the TOCs. Nevertheless Steven Norris told Christian Wolmar[41] that 'History will say that rail privatisation was one of the great privatisation successes'.

---

[41] *Ibid.*, p. 138.

Table 3 Performance of the Passenger Transport Industry,
1952-1998
Billions of passenger kilometres
(and percentages of total passenger kilometres, in brackets)

Year	Buses and coaches	Cars and vans	All road[a]	Rail	Car-owning households (%)
1952	92 (42)	58 (27)	180 (82)	39 (18)	
1957	84 (34)	92 (38)	201 (83)	42 (17)	22
1962	74 (25)	171 (57)	264 (87)	37 (12)	33
1967	66 (17)	267 (70)	345 (91)	34 (9)	47
1972	60 (14)	327 (76)	395 (91)	35 (8)	53
1977	58 (13)	354 (77)	425 (92)	34 (7)	56
1982	48 (10)	406 (81)	470 (93)	31 (6)	59
1987	47 (8)	500 (83)	560 (93)	40 (7)	64
1992	43 (6)	587 (86)	640 (94)	38 (6)	69
1993	43 (6)	585 (86)	637 (94)	37 (5)	69
1994	43 (6)	596 (87)	648 (94)	35 (5)	69
1995	44 (6)	596 (86)	648 (94)	36 (5)	70
1996	44 (6)	606 (86)	658 (94)	38 (5)	70
1997	44 (6)	614 (86)	666 (93)	41 (6)	70
1998	43 (6)	616 (86)	667 (93)	42 (6)	72

[a] Includes also motor and pedal cycles.

The decline in bus and coach traffic will be seen to be far more than offset by the growth in private car use. The rate of reduction has fallen markedly since 1987. The carryings of the railways were not seriously affected by the line and station closures of the mid-1960s, possibly due to the growth in commuting and a tendency for journeys to become longer.

Source – *Transport Statistics Great Britain 1999 Edition*, Government Statistical Service.

Leave Them Alone!

Writing in 1993, Stephen Glaister and Tony Travers showed remarkable foresight when they said 'The political nature of the privatisation process is hard to exaggerate'.[42]

---

[42] Stephen Glaister and Tony Travers, *New Directions for British Railways? – The Political Economy of Privatisation and Regulation*, London: IEA, 1993.

One plank in Labour's platform for the 1997 election was the re-nationalisation of the railways, supported with enthusiasm by John Prescott, and although the government has found this impossible (owing to the way privatisation had been designed), every effort is now being made to try to return to what in practice looks rather like the *ancien regime*.

Mr Prescott leaves us in no doubt that he wants to return the railways to control by central government. But although there are necessary reforms that would make the present complex system work better, the running of trains is a normal commercial activity, and, apart from safety control, requires a minimum of intervention to give economic efficiency and the effective satisfaction of demand. And improvements such as through ticketing and bus/rail links are already proceeding. Railway management has been through the biggest series of shocks of the entire twentieth century, and the need is to let the people who run the trains adjust to the disciplines of the market.

Structural reforms are another matter, and here the Strategic Rail Authority (SRA) may be able to help, provided it does not become a revived British Transport Commission. The evidence so far is that the Rail Regulator and the 'shadow' chairman of the SRA (who is also chairman of the continuing British Railways Board) have got the measure, for the time being, of the twin dangers of regulatory capture and political interference. But any form of state regulation, as John Blundell and Colin Robinson observe[43] must always be open to such risk, and who can rely on governments' self control to keep their fingers out?

Serious problems are already becoming plain as the expiry of the initial franchises comes closer, and the powers of the franchisor are to be transferred under the Bill to Sir Alastair Morton at the SRA and Mr Tom Winsor, the Rail Regulator. The element of confusion that lay at the heart of

---

[43] John Blundell and Colin Robinson, *Regulation Without the State*, Occasional Paper 109, London: IEA, 1999.

the initial legislation, whereby the TOCs were franchisees and not autonomous trading companies, could only lead to the problems of intervention from above. The responsibility rests with those who concluded that rail transport had an element of natural monopoly, so that the industry required to be governed in the same way as electricity, gas and telecommunications. Today it is even more urgently necessary to see that railways – and all forms of transport – are 'just another industry', that will flourish with a minimum degree of control and intervention by the state. Yet although major re-organisation is neither possible nor desirable, the 1999 rail disaster at Ladbroke Grove, with the subsequent political hysteria in the media, suggests that irrationality will continue to prevail.

London and the Channel

The future of the London Underground and the Channel Tunnel Link are subjects too often perceived to be detached from 'the railway problem'. Not only is this untrue, but neither of these matters can be dealt with as if they were independent.

London

London's transport, in particular, is bedevilled by history. Its urban railways consist of the London Transport network, which scarcely exists south of the Thames, and the former British Rail suburban lines. For many years the official underground map completely neglected the essential links provided by British Rail. State aid in the late 1930s and again after the war was used to extend London Transport trains over main-line tracks, thereby throwing a greater load on the central London network, which might well have been better left to function on its own. The consequence today is a boundary problem, for which a very imperfect solution has been devised.

Unwilling to contemplate outright privatisation, perhaps because of trade union problems, the government wants the private sector to take over the infrastructure, while leaving management of the train services in the hands of the *ancien regime*. But the state of London's railways, whether those of London Transport or the worst of the former British Rail lines, is so bad as to be a disgrace to the nation, and the cost of updating them should surely be borne by the authority that has let them fall into disrepair: government. London has the disadvantage compared with most of the world's great cities that, having pioneered the tubes, it has inherited a dated system. But that does not prevent the introduction of air-conditioning, or the modernisation of stations on both systems. The investment that is needed requires careful assessment before the efficiency of private sector management is brought to bear on it.

The government proposes to leave the operational side in the public sector; that is, with London Transport, the home of managerial inefficiency. Privatisation of the bus industry and of the former British Rail operations has showed how services can perfectly well continue to be operated after whole levels of management have been removed, and 55 Broadway (London Transport's one-time private sector headquarters in Westminster) is one of the last bastions of transport bureaucracy. With fewer people in offices and more staff on the stations, improving security and customer care, the London Underground would become a better place, but reforms like this can only come through privatisation. Trade unionists might not like the idea, but unless radical reform is undertaken the system will continue to deteriorate.

There is in fact a strong case for the infrastructure of the London Transport services becoming the responsibility of Railtrack, which already maintains parts of it where the track is shared with former British Rail trains. The individual Underground lines could then be identified for franchise, giving the operating companies concerned freedom to make improvements in quality. A clearing house would operate the ticketing system, allocating revenue according to journey; the present method of checking tickets at barriers lends itself to this. There would be a certain problem of boundary management, since the stations, although part of the infrastructure, should be included in the franchise to encourage improvements in quality and marketing, but it should not be impossible to find a solution to this. The government's present policy, which is a political compromise, with the track leased to a private company while train operation remains under public control, is a nonsense, making the worst of the situation.

There remains, though, the inheritance of indefensible under-funding that has brought London's railway system to the brink of breakdown. It is a far more serious problem than that inherited by the private sector from British Rail, and it demands urgent attention. From a number of sources (including Mr Livingstone) comes the suggestion that this should be dealt with by some form of bond issue, with direct government guarantees, similar to the arrangement for the Channel Tunnel fast link. Whether New Labour can commit itself to such a revolutionary change of policy must however be doubtful; yet anything else implies the continuance of something like the *status quo*.

The Channel Tunnel

The Channel Tunnel Link presents another aspect of political intervention, this time at its worst. One of the strange things about our attitude to the railways is that it is always the passenger trains that people want to play with. So the Channel Tunnel is seen as the *très chic* mode for a shopping trip to Paris, though many officials and business people continue to fly to Brussels, and the ferries retain their importance in the market. Investing vast sums to achieve a thirty-minute timesaving is of marginal value, when compared with the potential of the tunnel for freight, and the idea of using the links to develop a 'linear city' down the Thames estuary has nothing to do with the case. Furthermore, the farcical failure of the train company to make use of the train-sets it bought for through operations from the midlands and the north must be a standing reproach to its management.

When the railway from Ashford to Redhill was being built early in the nineteenth century, Brunel said to the civil engineer 'make a good job of it – the time will come when it will be needed for a Channel Tunnel'. Such foresight was totally lacking when plans for a new freight railway through the midlands, linked to this line, were 'talked out' in the House of Commons by four MPs whose seats were involved.[44] The project has now been restored to favour, and has Mr Prescott's personal blessing (though local opposition is still thought to be likely); but there remains a pressing need to rethink the purpose of the Tunnel for industry and the export-import business.

Conclusion – Where Should the Trains Go Now?

Mr Prescott says that his plans for the railways are the key to his dream of integration. They are not; unless it is integration from above that he means, and that is indeed a pipe-dream. Nevertheless, the 1993 legislation was something of the traditional dog's dinner, and *The Economist*, contemplating 'Britain's rotten railways' rightly observed that 'The culprit was not privatisation itself, but the haste with which it was done'.[45] That is true, but the policies of the present government have made confusion worse confused.

The first requirement must be a fundamental rethink of the function of the Strategic Rail Authority. At present it is an unnecessary level of administration, designed for political intervention. (At least the British Railways Board is to be wound up under the provisions of the Transport Bill). The franchising system should be progressively dismantled, as the TOCs succeed in meeting their terms and conditions; new franchises may be necessary as an interim measure. The TOCs should then own their rolling stock, and the ROSCOs should be wound up.

---

[44] Both the Ashford–Redhill line and the former Great Central Railway through the Midlands were built to 'Berne gauge', giving clearances that would permit the operation of continental wagons.

[45] *The Economist*, 3 July 1999.

A national clearing house should be set up, owned jointly by all the TOCs, to run the ticketing system, owning and managing the booking offices and arranging for sales through travel agents and the hospitality industry. Revenue would be divided out on a mileage basis, as is done with similar organisations to be found in the bus industry. The TOCs would still be able to offer promotional fares and group bookings for journeys over their own systems. Anti-competitive mergers should be watched over by the Office of Fair Trading, as they are for the bus industry.

But the most urgent reform concerns the method of payment to Railtrack for the use of the infrastructure. This is the very fulcrum round which the promotion of allocative efficiency must turn, and it is there that effectiveness can best be assured. Dr Gylee's recommendation[46] that payments should be on the basis of units of time, with punctuality analysis and consequent penalties, should be seriously examined; not least because it offers an opportunity of balancing the demands of the passenger and freight operators for limited resources. It would also provide a clear indication of the justification for investment in new and improved track, terminals and signalling.

Summing Up

As it stands, the government's Railways Bill is a recipe for confusion, leading to what has been called 'creeping renationalisation of the railways'.[47] The relationship between the Strategic Rail Authority, the Rail Regulator and the Health and Safety Executive would become blurred, and the ability of the market to ensure both efficiency and effectiveness would be severely curtailed. What is needed now is progress, but the government offers us the reverse.

---

[46] Presented at the PTRC Conference held at Robinson College, Cambridge, Cambridge, 17–19 September 1999.

[47] Denton Hall, quoted in *Transit* magazine, 113, 20 August 1999.

VI. Buses Facing Problems

There is a fairly general consensus now that the bus industry is more effective in a competitive regime than in the days of widespread public ownership and anti-competitive legislation. Those who would argue that the franchise system to be found in London (see p. 42) ought to be extended to the rest of the country are in a minority, and they have the conclusions of the industry, through its trade association,[48] ranged against them. One analyst, Andrew Evans,[49] questions the extent to which the market for a given route can be contestable in the long run, and raises the important and neglected issue of the pursuit of territorial monopoly by the larger business (in this, harking back to the 1930s). On the other hand, Professor Bradshaw, lately chairman of the independent Bus Appeals Body, has been quoted[50] as saying of the industry's behaviour: '. . . practitioners (are) offering at least two courses of treatment – a blue bottle labelled "competition" and marked "administer continuously", and red pills labelled "franchising". The blue bottle, he said, "purges the system of perceived evils such as high fares, complacent, unresponsive management, cross-subsidy, cartels, conspiracies against the customer and other perceived obstructions".' He remarked that its side

---

[48] The Conference of Passenger Transport UK.

[49] Andrew W. Evans, Are urban bus services natural monopolies?, *Transportation* 18, 1991, pp. 131–150.

[50] *Coach and Bus Week*, 27 April 1996.

effects laid the patient open to attacks of 'Mk.1 Leyland Nationalitis'.[51] The red franchising pills 'are known to bring on constipation and promote lethargy and lack of response to stimuli'. Professor Bradshaw's views on contestability were also those of the House of Commons Transport Committee,[52] where, after mentioning the danger of an operator with a *de facto* monopoly becoming complacent and abusing a position of market dominance, they go on to say

> We therefore believe there is a need to ensure that market entry is always feasible in order to deter such operators from ceasing to innovate or allowing costs and fares to rise.

No doubt some contestability is better than none, and the bus industry today is in remarkably better state than it was under public ownership and protectionist regulation at the end of the 1970s. The decline in sales that had set in by 1950, with the failure of management to recognise that the car, not their neighbouring operators, was their competitor, has effectively come to an end (see Table 2). True, there are substantial areas where the potential of marketing management has yet to be understood by bus companies, but this is offset by the recognition among the better ones that the supermarkets should provide their most effective benchmark.

Commercial road motor transport has been an embarrassing problem for all traditionalists throughout the twentieth century. Basically, the problem is how we pay for the roads, as we saw in Chapter 3, A Market for Road Space, but it is also cultural. Traditionally, railway undertakings have been role cultures (in Handy's analysis), whereas the typical bus or truck firm is a power culture, putting success before

---

[51] The Leyland National was a bus designed and built to be the the the ideal public service vehicle. In this it failed, and was phased out by the larger companies after 1986, only to 'cascade' down to small businesses at the lower cost. Although sturdy, it is not a good advertisement for the bus industry as it seeks to move up market.

[52] Session 1995–96, First Report, *The Consequences of Bus Deregulation*, Volume 1, HMSO, p.liii.

structure or regulation. And their vehicles can come and go over the whole system without the constraint of having to run on rails. Railwaymen in the past have tended to act as if they were alone in the market.

The attitude runs through much of public debate. In terms of volume of traffic, railways are certainly of minor importance (see Table 3), but you would not know it from the media. There are, we may suppose, millions of people in Britain who have never travelled by train, but how many of those who think bus deregulation was a disaster have ever travelled by bus?

The Transport Act of 1985 set out to deregulate the bus industry, but it did more. Kevin Hey has recorded the origins and development of the argument for deregulation,[53] and it is fair to say that those of us who had defended the measure over the years[54] had failed to give adequate thought to the privatisation that was included in the Bill.

The Act provided a carefully prepared timetable for deregulation, but there was nothing comparable for the privatisation side. HM Treasury had originally pressed for the straight sale of the National Bus Company and (against resistance from north of the Border) of the Scottish Bus Group. But Mr Ridley was persuaded that deregulation in such a case would be meaningless, and (as we saw in Chapter 4) the subsidiaries of the two state-owned holding companies were sold separately. The early sales and management buy-outs (MBOs) were undervalued, but at the completion of the sale the Treasury received more than it had expected from its original policy.

---

[53] Kevin Hay, The story of bus deregulation, *Proceedings of the Chartered Institute of Transport*, 7(4), 1999, pp. 17–40.

[54] My own MSc thesis of 1954 (unpublished) was the basis for my Hobart Paper 23, *Transport for Passengers* (1963), and much of my argument was reflected in the Bill. The lapse of time from 1954 to 1984 may remind the reader that Keynes once remarked that it takes thirty years for a new idea to work its way through the political system. Nevertheless, I prize a copy of the Act, signed by the Secretary of State, Nicholas Ridley.

The lack of a timetable for privatisation made the process highly political. The difficulty lay, not in the nationalised part of the business, but in the metropolitan counties, and the Greater Glasgow Region (Strathclyde), along with some of the municipal undertakings. It was the in these areas that the problems chiefly arose.

The metropolitan counties and Strathclyde had inherited the provisions of the Transport Act 1968, and were Passenger Transport Authorities (PTAs) in their own right, each with a Passenger Transport Executive (PTE) which, among other things, operated the buses and contracted with British Rail to run the trains (other than the Tyneside Metro, which was run by the PTE).[55] The PTEs became, in effect, municipal transport committees, with all the problems of public-choice theory attached. They tended also to develop into overstaffed bureaucracies. The 1985 Act required them to be converted into joint-stock companies (as it did for the other municipal transport committees), with a view to sale; the council and one or two officers being the shareholders. By 1985, however, the PTAs were all set in Labour-controlled authorities, which were strongly opposed to the new legislation.

The period between the 1968 and 1985 Acts saw the continued decline in passenger traffic (see Table 2), combined with the rapid increase in state and municipal subsidy referred to above (p. 38). This declining efficiency was matched by the failure of the PTEs to provide the services that the majority of people wanted. But the impact of deregulation was not be avoided, and the reactions of the PTEs varied according to the political reaction of the county councils – even though they were to be dissolved at this time under local government reform. One council is

---

[55] In this the 1968 Act departed drastically from the previous White Paper, which had envisaged Conurbation Transport Authorities, with planning and co-ordinating but not operational responsibility. Their objective was to have been the integration of land-use and transport planning, but powers for this were not given to the PTAs. For some examples of the consequent weaknesses see my paper *Trouble with the Authorities*, London: Adam Smith Institute, 1998.

said to have instructed its officers that they were to ignore the forthcoming changes, and make no plans for the commercialised future that awaited them; even that they were to make the deregulated regime unworkable. Yet it will be obvious that the structure of the industry after 1985 was far removed from the pattern of small, competitive firms that Mr Ridley is said to have envisaged.

The one thing that is plain from hindsight is that some PTEs were better than others in facing the new dispensation. Thus the West Midlands PTE was able to retain more than 90% of its services, whereas the Greater Manchester and Merseyside executives seem to have panicked, dropping considerable mileage, and thus inviting new competitors to enter the market. So people in the West Midlands noticed little change, whereas in the north- west there was chaos. The experience seems to suggest a failure to appreciate the value of contributory revenue arising from mileage that more than covers its escapable costs; a mistake that was avoided in the West Midlands. Ponsonby had demonstrated this as early as 1963.[56] Little attention seems to have been paid in some of the PTEs to the report on cross-subsidy in urban bus operations published jointly by the National Bus Company and the University of Leeds Institute for Transport Studies in March 1984.

The outcome was the politicisation of the whole programme of reform. Attention focused on the strongly left-leaning PTAs,[57] ignoring successes elsewhere. For example, to the south of Greater Manchester lies the conurbation known as the Potteries, served by the formerly state-owned company Potteries Motor Traction, initially a management buy-out firm. Using the modified route licensing system introduced by the Transport Act 1980, and with few competitors to object, by deregulation's D-day the company's services had already been adapted to meet the

---

[56] G. J. Ponsonby, What is an unremunerative service?, *Institute of Transport Journal*, 1963.

[57] It seems that very few councillors from other political parties differed from the Labour majorities in the PTAs.

new regime, and it is doubtful whether local people noticed any change. The Greater Manchester PTE could perfectly well have done the same.

Unfortunately the experiences in certain of the PTEs, notably Greater Manchester, Merseyside and Tyne & Wear, commanded attention to such an extent as to damn the whole process by association, with the 'progressive' (left-wing and trade union) commentators making the most of it. Because nothing spectacular happened in the West Midlands and many other parts of the country, the successes of the reform were not news. A short-lived confrontation in Glasgow was criticised, despite the fact that both parties at the time were still in public ownership, and the Traffic Commissioner attributed the congestion to the private car. But it was in what used to be called the 'Socialist Republic of South Yorkshire' that the greatest political upheaval threatened. As Passenger Transport Authority, the Metropolitan County Council had decided to phase out fares, apparently on the argument that so many more people would use the buses and trains that the council could save on its highways estimates. Although the complete 'fares-free' objective was never reached, the 1985 Act required the PTE to raise its prices by more than 200 per cent. The expected revolution never took place.

The industry since 1985 has seen a steady concentration of ownership, in which a number of progressive and innovative groups have been swallowed up by the larger holding companies; a process comparable with that of the 1930s. The truth seems to be that these companies have sought growth by acquisition, perhaps because the encouragement of organic growth is more challenging, but also because their financial backers may not always have grasped the commercial potential of the industry if management is permitted to invest for expansion. It is interesting that the business consistently awarded the accolade as the UK's Best Bus Company[58] is independent of

---

[58] Trent and Barton Buses, of Heanor, Derbyshire. For more details see Box 2, p. 76.

any ownership group.

Most informed opinion today accepts that the regulatory reform and restructuring of the bus industry was necessary, and has been, on balance, a success, and the statistics support this (Table 2). Although numbers carried continued for a time to decrease, the takeover process slowed down, and has virtually ceased. Moreover, the more market-oriented companies, all over Britain, have significantly out-performed the aggregate.

Two Crisis Points

Setting aside the issue of franchise, which we examined and rejected in Chapter 4, the bus industry today is a largely successful enterprise, whose managers have turned it round from the period of 'managed decline' that began in the 1950s, but have not been allowed to revert to the big company and municipality cartel that dominated the period before nationalisation. They themselves admit that the threat of competition is something they would not want to lose, since it provides the continued incentive to respond to the market that had been removed in 1930. But there are two major problems that have still to be resolved.

The Problem of Price

Over the thirty years prior to the removal of price control in 1980 the fares charged by the bus industry were required by the Traffic Commissioners to reflect internal cross-subsidy, and were based on fully allocated average cost per mile. As my own research showed,[59] any change was slow in coming. The average cost base contributed also to the long period of decline, which I have called 'the strange suicide of the British bus industry', as contributory revenue was sacrificed by cutting out so-called 'loss-making mileage'. The example of Greater Manchester outlined above was a tragic outcome of this mistaken approach;

---

[59] John Hibbs, An evaluation of urban bus deregulation in Britain: a survey of management attitudes, *Progress in Planning*, 36(3), 1991, pp. 163–257.

Table 4 Vehicle Miles and Subsidy Payments, 1985-1997

Year	Local bus services (vehicle kilometres)	Public transport support (£million at 1996/97 prices)
1985/86	2,007	792
1986/87	2,160	681[a]
1987/88	2,342	524[a]
1988/89	2,390	485[a]
1989/90	2,442	390[a]
1990/91	2,448	396[a]
1991/92	2,488	455
1992/93	2,515	440
1993/94	2,585	277[b]
1994/95	2,649	287[b]
1995/96	2,623	271[b]
1996/97	2,693	254[b]
Percentage change over 11 years	+34	-68

[a] Includes Rural Bus Grant.

[b] Public transport support in 1993/94 was affected by changes in London in preparation for the privatisation of London Transport Buses; and in 1994/95, 1995/96 and 1996/97 public transport support in London was internally funded by London Transport with no direct revenue support from central government. 1996/97 figure is provisional.

Source: *Transport Statistics Report – Bus and Coach Statistics Great Britain* 1996/97. Government Statistical Service.

The figures show the substantial growth of output by the bus industry, for local bus services, since the Transport Act 1985, and the even more striking reduction in public expense. The remaining support is targeted towards services not provided commercially, after competitive tendering procedures.

perhaps the last blow dealt to the prosperity of the industry by the Road Traffic Act 1930.

The inevitable outcome of a pricing policy unrelated to the market has been the situation today: bus fares have for far too long been too low to permit a higher standard of the quality of the product. Despite the extension of market-based pricing, encouraged by competition from small firms with lower costs, there is much truth in this today. But to advocate higher prices is to come up against the argument of many planners and politicians, echoed in the media, that only lower fares will encourage car users to 'return to public transport'.

Many firms in the bus industry today have faced this problem, and have introduced more flexible charges, with discriminatory fares in the off-peak and so on. And as we shall see when we examine the problem of wages, great improvements in quality have come from substantial new investment. Fares have in fact risen generally faster than the cost of living (Table 5), and this has attracted criticism, whereas it has been an inescapable consequence of the

Table 5 Changes in Bus Fares Compared with the Retail Price Index 1987-1998 (1995=100)

Year	Fare index (outside London)	Retail price index
1987/98	62.7	68.9
1998/89	65.9	73.0
1989/90	70.9	78.7
1990/91	78.0	86.4
1991/92	84.8	90.5
1992/93	89.4	93.3
1993/94	92.8	94.9
1994/95	96.8	97.5
1995/96	101.2	100.7
1996/97	106.6	103.1
1997/98	112.8	106.5

Figures for Wales before 1992/93 are omitted as insufficient fares data were available.

Source: *Transport Statistics Great Britain* 1999 Edition, Government Statistical Service.

The recent upward trend can be accounted for by the substantially increased investment, and its effects on passenger carryings appear to have been negligible.

return of the industry to the market economy, and all the benefits that have followed.

One experiment that has shown some success has been the operation of services at different levels of quality, with different fares, along the same route. Pioneered by Stagecoach in Manchester, with the proviso that there must be sufficient strength of demand to justify it, reports indicate a growth of traffic and revenue on both the 'state of art' services and the 'Magicbus' cheaper alternative (Box 1). Market segmentation has been shown to work, but in the absence of some form of road-use pricing there is currently no opportunity for the same process at the upper end of the market.

Box 1 Magicbus

Among the earlier marketing initiatives of the Stagecoach Group was Brian Souter's 'cheap and cheerful' Magicbus network in Glasgow. More recently the brand name has been used for the successful development of market segmentation, first in south Manchester and then in other companies in the group. While modern, sophisticated buses continue to run on the main roads concerned, older vehicles also operate, as Magicbus, at lower fares. Contrary to the conventional wisdom, passengers do discriminate, so long as the frequency is high enough, so that both levels of service are financially justified. Price discrimination, prohibited by the licensing system from 1930 to 1980, has been shown to have a place in a mature industry like today's bus services, and it has appeared on busy routes in many cities on a competitive basis. Souter stresses that only the busiest routes can carry more than one service, and it is problematic how far upward price discrimination would succeed in the face of car competition – though road-use pricing might make enough difference to make it possible.

There is reason to believe that the existence of alternatives encourages demand, as it does in the retail trades. This is a further argument for the retention of a contestable market. But it is true that the highest standards of operation and marketing are not everywhere to be found. What is more, margins are tight, and some of the smaller firms are using buses that give the whole industry a bad name. To argue for lower fares makes no sense, though, and to introduce them by way of subsidy would invite a return to the weaknesses of the past, where contestability would be ruled out, along with the healthy profit-seeking that makes for effective satisfaction. Even so, there are those who advocate the use of funds from road-pricing to offer a 'cheaper alternative'. That would be a disaster.

The Problem of Wages

The drastic reductions in operating cost that followed privatisation were largely achieved by de-layering management and introducing plant bargaining in place of the national agreements formerly negotiated centrally with the trade unions. But this policy has now long run its course, while the opportunities to achieve economies of scope by purchase are now very few. If the industry is to continue to please the City, other than by overseas investment, it must be through organic growth; a new maturity has been reached, in which the window of opportunity for new entrants on any scale no longer exists.

Much effort and some success has been seen in the considerable investment that has gone into new and user-friendly vehicles, strongly encouraged by the government. Local authorities have helped by developing Quality Partnerships, with the provision of bus priority lanes, improved kerbing at bus stops, with better waiting accommodation[60] and 'real time' information. But several companies had already broken new ground by training their drivers in customer-care; skills that bus drivers, unlike the conductors of past days, were not famous for (Box 2). Some impressive gains have come from developments of this kind, but the problem remains of how to attract and retain staff during a period of low unemployment.

---

[60] It is a standing joke that you can't get a bus into a 'bus shelter'.

Box 2 Rainbows Over the Midlands

Trent and Barton Buses, based at Heanor in Derbyshire, and owned entirely by employees, retired employees and their families, is well known in the industry for its pioneering development of customer-friendly, market researched and branded services, so much so that the company has received a string of awards:

- 1st Bus Good Practice Award 1992
- 1st Bus Good Practice Award 1993
- 1st First Direct/Daily Telegraph Customer First Award 1994
- 1st Bus Industry Innovation Award 1996
- 1st National Federation of Bus Users Welcome Aboard 'UK's Best Bus Company' 1996
- 'Bus Operator of the Year Award' 1999 'Marketing Initiative Award' 1999

Much of this stems from the company's Rainbow Routes, which were initially developed on the Derby-Nottingham corridor. A fleet of new buses, with specially trained drivers and an effective' customer's charter, with improved marketing for the brand, led to immediate increases in traffic. One of the company's first top quality services experienced above 5% pa passenger growth in its first four years. Another striking achievement was the Spondon Flyer, launched in 1994 after intensive customer research, where carryings have continued to grow, and, astonishingly, 70% of a researched sample of former motorists are now using the bus. The company is firmly opposed to the policy of franchise, which would replace marketing initiatives like these with 'bland mediocrity determined by bureaucrats some steps removed from the customer'.

With acknowledgements to the company's response to the 1997 Green Paper, *Developing an integrated transport policy – An invitation to contribute.*

It seems that wages are too low to recruit and hold drivers of the character best attuned to customer-care skills – skills which perhaps should not need to be taught. Organic growth can best come from quality, and drivers are at least as important as state-of-the-art vehicles in assuring this. But it is not just the drivers whose skills deserve attention; the development of systemic thought throughout the staff is capable of turning the business into a learning organisation, and setting it on the road to growth and greater prosperity.[61] But to do this takes time, and if your shareholders or backers are looking for an immediate 20%, you do not have it.

A serious problem exists, though, in the regulations governing recruitment and training of drivers. The President of the Confederation of Passenger Transport has spoken of the 'bizarre administrative barriers' that, for example, affect the issue of provisional licences for bus drivers. In this way and in others the industry today, far from being 'deregulated', is subject to greater intervention than it has suffered from at any time in the past.

Strengths and Weaknesses

The maturity of the bus industry today must not blind us to the variety of standards that exist, or to the remaining problems of local government intervention. Greater Manchester has settled down well, with two leading companies and a number of small firms, most of which have high standards of quality. Oxford is a good example of the benefits of competition – despite what can only be described as a 'hatchet job' by the BBC (see Box 5) in a programme in November 1999. But there are still too many companies, large and small, members of groups or independents, whose managers have yet to learn the lesson of the market: that their business is carrying people, not running buses. There is little evidence from the trade journals of an understanding of marketing management; of market research or market intelligence.[62] It would seem that much of what passes for marketing in the industry is not much more than advertising and promotion. And although contestability is widely accepted as a necessary condition for progress, there are parts of the country where there is evidence of the worst excesses of competition.

Perhaps more serious, though, is the behaviour of some local authorities, seeking to re-establish their control over

---

[61] See for example Peter M. Senge, *The Fifth Discipline – The Art and Practice of The Learning Organization*, London: Century Business, 1990.

[62] I have argued elsewhere against the development of a marketing department in a bus company.

the bus services. On the one hand this can range from the pettifogging enforcement of stand-times, with fines for staying a minute over the authorised time, to policies like those of Birmingham City Council, which appears to intend to remove buses (but not trams) from central area streets entirely And there is a general distrust of the smaller firms, however valuable their lower operating costs may be when it comes to spending public money for tendered services. After all, the lower fares charged by a small firm may be just what the passenger in the poorer parts of the city appreciates.

Ultimately it is the drivers – the point-of-sale staff – who make or break the bus company, and customer care is increasingly emphasised. But the further step, of giving a financial incentive to the driver, which is to be seen in the route associations in cities like Buenos Aires, has made little headway here. It is sad to relate that a proposal in the early 1980s for high-frequency minibus services across London by such an association, vehemently opposed by both London Transport and the National Bus Company, was turned down by the Licensing Authority, whose decision was upheld on appeal by Nicholas Ridley.

Quality: Assured or Imposed?

In recent years a new arrangement has appeared, the Quality Partnership. Conceptually, the partnership is between commercial and local government interests, with, ideally, the police being involved where enforcement is required. Where there is a Passenger Transport Authority its Executive (the PTE) will also be a party to the agreements. In one classic case, Birmingham's Line 33, the parties were Travel West Midlands (TWM), the city council as highway authority (along with Walsall council, since the route just enters that borough), the West Midlands PTE and the West Midlands Police Force. Its success has been outstanding, and similar 'showcase' projects have followed. One of them, between Walsall and Bloxwich, originated from the initiative of a local firm, Choice Travel, which runs in partnership with TWM, Walsall council and the PTE.

But public money is involved in such partnerships, and local government finance works to different rules, as we shall see when we look at light rapid transit. Some local authorities have been pressing for the bus company to make a contribution to the costs of their schemes, and some bus companies have been tempted to go along with this. Others have sought to ban the use of the designated stopping places by companies outwith the partnership. Thus a situation appears to be arising in which property rights are becoming established in the highway. (Klein, Moore and Reja see this as a way to retain contestability and a place for the 'jitney' – Box 3). There is the danger of a boundary of some importance being crossed here, inasmuch as the local authority has a duty to provide for all road-users out of the general fund of taxable income.

Box 3 Kerb Rights

In a rigorous analysis of the economics of 'transit', Klein, Moore and Reja look at the British experience of deregulation. Their comments and recommendations are worthy of serious thought. Remarking that 'The clearest winners . . . are British taxpayers' they continue

The central failing of British bus deregulation is the difficulty that bus companies have had in appropriating their investment in waiting passengers. The result has been schedule jockeying and route swamping, which has disrupted service and diminished competitiveness in the industry. Once again there is deficiency in the property rights framework leading to a tendency toward monopoly.

They recommend the introduction of curb rights (US spelling). Although they regard the British system with favour (as do a number of other US commentators), they fear that full contestability can be destructive, where an established operator might be put out of business by competitors. Their answer is to give operators of scheduled services property rights, in the form of exclusive rights to set down and pick up passengers along designated lengths of kerb. Their approach may be foreign to British bureaucratic thinking, and quite foreign to the proposed 'quality contracts', but it should be widely read and experimented with.

See Daniel B. Klein, Adrian T. Moore and Binyam Reja, *Curb Rights – A Foundation for Free Enterprise in Urban Transit*, Washington DC: Brookings Institution Press, 1997.

The point of principle here is this: so soon as a financial deal of this kind is set up, the Quality *Partnership* starts to look like a Quality *Contract*. And it is just this that is provided for in the Transport Bill. It is seen as a follow-on where a partnership (for some unstated reason) is seen to fail. In the case of a Quality Partnership, the bus company's input of quality is voluntary (if for perfectly proper self-seeking reasons), and negotiable. In the case of a Quality Contract, the tendency would be for the public sector planners to determine the quality input from the bus company – and to enforce the contract in such a way as to deny contestability. Such control could then extend to such matters as timetables and fares.

The Quality Contract can only appear as the first step toward the allocation of a *franchise*, and thus a more towards re-regulation. We have already seen that this is a dangerous road to tread (Chapter 4). For although most informed opinion today argues that a return to bureaucracy in the provision of bus transport would be a recipe for deficits and disaster, there is a hankering in certain quarters for power to return to the public sector. The argument that the London system of franchise is superior to the relatively open market elsewhere in Britain is spurious; London bus managers are not allowed to practice any form of marketing management of the kind that places the consumer first.[63] There is indeed a very strong argument for completing the task left unfinished by the late Conservative government, and 'deregulating' the London bus market, winding up at the same time the vast and unwieldy London Buses/London Transport bureaucracy; yet, instead, we now see London Transport setting itself up once again as a bus operator, in competition with the very companies that it franchises, while the Mayor issues new instructions that handcuff the company managers still more.

---

[63] See John Hibbs, *Don't Stop the Bus*, London: Adam Smith Institute, 1999.

The Return of the Tram

There is a form of urban passenger transport to be found in American and continental cities known today as light rapid transit (LRT), which has been introduced in a few places in this country, with decidedly mixed results. A neologism that is hard to pin down, it may appear as the resurrection of the electric tramcar of enthusiasts' delight, or as a form of railed transport slightly lower in status than 'heavy rail'.

Because it uses electricity for power, LRT is regarded as superior to the supposedly polluting diesel bus. (To an extent, of course, it puts the pollution back to the power station.) Because it is new investment, its state-of-the-art vehicles are supposed to be more attractive to passengers, though the successes of Quality Partnerships and good marketing management show what the bus is still able to achieve. But before we go on to analyse its disadvantages, the fact must be faced that it offers an opportunity for local government officials and councillors to get back into the passenger transport market by proxy. Many millions of pounds have been spent in assessing proposals for LRT investment, sometimes in the most unlikely places, scarcely any of which have been able to pass HM Treasury's justified limits on public spending. And not a little money has gone into trips to foreign cities, for councillors to inspect modern tramcars offering services at the cost of heavy subsidy.

The greatest single weakness of the argument for LRT lies in the very high level of capital spending required, in comparison with investment in the infrastructure of the bus industry. A modern tramway requires new depots, new vehicles, power supply, 'stations', if it is to make use of a former 'heavy rail' line, and miles of steel track. If there is to be 'street running', there will be the costs imposed on road users and traders during the period of construction. Buses, on the other hand, exist already and, even if new, are far cheaper than tramcars; they do not need new depots, or power supply, and they use existing 'track'. Even if this is to be improved, by dedicated bus lanes or sections of kerb-guided track (Box 4), the costs involved are far less than those required for the trams.[64]

Box 4 KGB – a Better Choice than Trams

Urban transport policy in Britain today carries a certain politically correct notion that buses are by their nature downmarket, and that wherever possible they should be replaced by trams. Because the trams, which expired in the 1960s except at Blackpool, had a remarkably downmarket image of their own, their successors are correctly referred to as light rapid transit (LRT). Modelled on state-of-the-art tramway systems that have been built or expanded at great public expense in many cities in Europe, they attracted so much attention in the early 1990s that numerous schemes were proposed, and studies commissioned at public expense, in places as widespread as Glasgow and Gloucester, most of them turning the proposition down. Since then the success of quality partnerships such as the *Line 33* project in the West Midlands has shown that the bus can attract demand far more effectively than had been assumed (and see also Box 3), and HM Treasury has become very cautious about permitting public investment in LRT (the financial disaster of the Sheffield *Supertram* playing a great part in this).

There is, however, a far more attractive way of obtaining the advantages claimed for LRT in terms of lapsed time, and one which is very much more economical of both finance and land-take. This is *kerb guided bus* (KGB). The principle is simple. A concrete track is laid, where there is a congestion problem, of the width necessary for the wheels of the bus to fit it, and made inaccessible to other vehicles. Low down at the side of the bus is a wheel which bears on the kerb and thus controls the steering of the vehicle along the busway. In this way the bus has all the advantages of the tram, but at vastly less expense, and with other benefits as well. The guidewheel is inexpensive; the bus exists already and does not have to be built as an extremely costly tram would; no rails or overhead electric wiring are needed; no power needs to be distributed to the track; and, finally, there is no need to construct elaborate new depots, with maintenance facilities and so forth. And whereas the tram is confined to its tracks, the bus service can continue to penetrate the housing areas, many of whose residents would need to walk to the tram stop, instead of having the bus more or less

---

[64] A much neglected alternative is the system of busways built during the expansion of the north-west town of Runcorn in the 1970s. These may be used by more than one operator, with no special equipment needed on the bus; they are convenient for housing, and lead into a covered bus station in the shopping centre.

outside. KGB sections have been introduced in various places – notably Ipswich and Leeds – with great success, yet there still seems to be an assumption that LRT is preferable to KGB – maybe because KGB is distinctly 'low-tech'. (Another reason may be that local authorities, having lost control of public transport after deregulation, seek to get it back by building tramways.) (For further information, see 'Privatisation and Innovation – Exploiting Guided Bus', by Bob Tebb, in the *Proceedings of the Chartered Institute of Transport* 6(4), December 1997, pp. 42-49). However, a new development, gratifyingly 'high-tech', which promises to reduce the cost of guided busway systems, is the CIVIS hybrid-engined vehicle, which uses computer-assisted optical routing – it follows a line painted on the road surface. (The hybrid engine has a light diesel power unit to feed current to wheel-mounted electric motors.) A 26 km route is to be constructed in Rouen. The vehicles can of course 'fan out' at the end of the guided section, to serve suburban streets, which is notoriously impossible for the LRT trams.

But ultimately, in terms of effective consumer satisfaction, the bus has one great advantage over the tram: it does not have to be *trackbound*. Only the bus can offer point-to-point travel, from home to shops or work or entertainment, without the need to change *en route*, as many people must who have to use the tram. Kerb-guided buses can still serve suburban communities while gaining the advantage of priority in congested streets, an advantage that has always been denied to trams and trolleybuses alike. And the temptation to restructure bus services to advantage the trams is a further risk that the market would be destabilised.

If it is conceded that concentrations of demand may exist such that the unit cost of railed transport can be lowered enough to make LRT or heavy rail a justified investment, the demand forecasts must still be treated with reserve, because of the elements of fashion and municipal pride that will inevitably exist. The financial failure of the Sheffield Supertram system stands as a warning; there, for political reasons, the track was laid to serve poorer districts where people could not afford the high fares necessitated by the costly enterprise. The concept was undermined by the demands of the highway engineers, who saw themselves as both contractor and client, and as guardians of the road space. The consequent financial burden for the local authorities of South Yorkshire, since HM Treasury would not bail them out, has been extremely serious.

Other weaknesses follow from the use of abandoned railway lines (usually abandoned for good reason), as American experience has demonstrated. Ian Yearsley has shown[65] that a prime cause of the disappearance of the electric tram from British cities lay in the nature of local government finance, such that renewal funds were simply not available as the systems came to the end of their useful lives. He raises the question 'Will there be a political desire *and the financial means* [italics added] to renew the new generation of light rail systems in, say, the year 2024?' And he concludes

> If light rail is to develop and prosper in this country, there is a question about renewals to be addressed. It was, after all, at the financial heart of the decline of the previous generation of tramways.

The Coaching Trade

In any hierarchy of esteem the coach is likely to rank lower than the bus, despite the fact that coaches are generally more comfortable than buses and are used by many senior people in business and public life who probably never use a bus; coaches are used to move parties of distinguished guests from place to place.

This important branch of the public transport industry falls into three parts –

- the network of *long-distance express coach services*[66] that covers Great Britain, dominated in England and Wales by the National Express company, together with the commuter coach services largely to be found serving London, and the services to and from airports;

---

[65] Ian Yearsley, Light rail – who pays? *Proceedings of the Chartered Institute of Transport*, 5(2), 1996, pp. 3–12.

[66] This sector was relieved of licensing control (other than for safety) by the Transport Act 1980. Neil Douglas (in *A Welfare Assessment of Transport Deregulation*, London: Gower, 1987) concluded that, allowing for the incentive for improved rail services, 'deregulation (had) led to an improvement in social welfare'.

- *the coach holiday traffic*, where three large firms share the market with innumerable smaller ones; this includes a considerable movement of overseas tourists, many from the USA, on package holidays; the industry provides for tourist expenditure of some £2 billion a year, and coach-based tourism generates 80,000 jobs;
- *the coaching trade proper*, consisting of small firms, often family businesses owning a few vehicles only, most of whose work is in the charter, or private hire market, or in sub-contracting to tourism firms; but who may also be working tendered 'bus' services for local councils, for schoolchildren or for more general traffic.

Much coach operation caters for people on a low income, and it is specially important in areas where rail services are poor. The dismissive attitude of government to this part of the industry is quite unjustified. Thus, under an EU ruling in 1999 coach speeds were limited to 62 mph (100 km/h). In 1992 heavy goods vehicles over 12 tonnes were subjected to a speed limit of 52.8 mph (85 km/h), and the subsequent banning of coaches from the outside lane of six-lane motorways tended to trap them amidst the slower-moving goods vehicles, yet the British government sought no dispensation for vehicles that had been operated safely for so many years with a 70 mph limit on motorways and other dual carriageways.

These examples of government attitudes, however, are small by comparison with the refusal of HM Treasury to allow the fuel duty rebate that applies to bus services to be extended to coaches, whether on regular or charter operation. Coach services and the charter operators provide an important contribution to the movement of people, and it is surely discriminatory for senior citizens' passes not to be available for passengers from country villages going by coach to a bingo hall, or on a Christmas shopping excursion. The tourism industry is dependent on the coaching trade, and tourist resorts and attractions are dependent on tourism. The distinction between a bus service and a coach service is largely one of bureaucratic convenience, and means nothing to the passenger.

Even the regulatory framework can be politically correct. Pressure to provide (and even to 'retrofit') seatbelts for vehicles carrying schoolchildren has failed to recognise the difficulty of enforcing their use, except by an attendant, whose wages would double the labour costs involved. In any case, many firms have ceased to tender for this work, because of the damage they have suffered from uncontrolled schoolchildren. Then there is the effect on costs of requiring wheelchair access, especially for double-deck and high-floor coaches used for long distance services and tours respectively.

To be blunt, there is prejudice here, of two kinds. The first is the image of 'coach trips' as something rather inferior to going by train or using the car; like much prejudice, this is entirely unjustified. But the second is more peculiar: it is a politically motivated dislike of the small firm, itself arising from two sources: the tidy administrative mind, and the inability of trade unions to organise the trade.

Small firms in the bus industry offend the tidy minds of administrators, though their importance for the tendered 'socially necessary' services and school contracts means the bureaucrats have to live with them. Even in the cities, though, the distinction between bus and coach businesses is often unclear at this level, and a rural operator will mix charter work with tendered or commercial bus services, to maximise turnover. What matters here is in the nature of the coaching trade itself.

Coach drivers form an elite in the industry. As in all service industries there are non-monetary satisfactions involved in customer care (quite apart from the traditional tip), one of which arises from the responsibility the driver takes for the safety and satisfaction of the passengers, and another from the skills inherent in the driving itself. Many small firms in the trade are of the nature of a *gemeinschaft*,[67] so that drivers identify themselves with the business to an

---

[67] See Michael Baines, Implications of organisational complexity for local bus operations, *Proceedings of the Chartered Institute of Transport*, 7(2), June 1998.

extent that is much less likely to be found in the *gesellschaft*, character of the large bus company. As well as this, the coach driver's job is relatively isolated, which may encourage a certain independence of mind. But whatever the reasons, the trade unions have never been able to organise the coaching trade in the way they came to dominate the bus industry by the 1950s. Not surprisingly, then, the coach operators, large and small, feel that they are not given the status they deserve in the eyes of policy-makers. It is true to say that they suffer from an unjustified discrimination, and it should be a priority of both DETR and HM Treasury to set this right.

Summing Up

The bus and coach industry has shown since the reforms of the 1980s that it can break free from political control, seeking and satisfying demand that had existed long before. The system of regulation is unnecessarily complex, and the intervention of local authorities is particularly to be criticised. Both in this and to encourage the allocative efficiency of the industry the commercial freedom of bus managers must be widened, especially in London, where deregulation is urgently required. The coaching trade deserves better of the system, and should be treated more equitably. But it is a matter of the highest priority to reject any trend to franchise, and therefore to the introduction of Quality Contracts.

VII. The Rural Problem

What *is* the Countryside?

Britain is a highly urbanised country. It thus contains large areas that are relatively underpopulated. The problems arising from this have become progressively more acute since the late 1940s; so much so that the reality of the 'countryside', as a social concept, bears very little relationship to the impression of the typical city-dweller. So in transport terms, strange as it may seem, the political issues are not very far removed from those concerning fox-hunting, and are closely linked to tourism as a 'consumer of heritage'.

The problems have been systematically neglected, and are little understood from the urban political standpoint. The Jack Committee reported 38 years ago,[68] but its recommendations had no noticeable effect on policy. What was already plain was the impact of mechanisation on arable farming and the consequent flight of labour to find work in the towns. In country lanes today no evidence remains of many cottages that have been abandoned, while others have been made over into holiday retreats or the homes of middle-class commuters.

The first difficulty in dealing with the problem is that of definition. Short of creating a pattern from the civil parishes, local authority boundaries mean little, so throwing funds at the problem is very inaccurate. But there is a second complication, arising from the nature of settlement, which affects the extent to which bus services can be commercially viable. Nucleated villages along or near a

---

[68] *Report of the Committee on Rural Bus Services*, chaired by Professor D. T. Jack, HMSO, 1961. There was a concomitant report on Bus Services in the Highlands and Islands, HMSO, 1961, which was no doubt equally neglected.

main road between towns can be easily served on a regular, daily basis, but areas of scattered settlement have always had to put up with more irregular services. The accident of railway construction in the nineteenth century meant that only a limited number of villages ever had train services, and since the 1920s the bus has been the only serious provider of rural public transport.

The 1950s saw the 'golden age' of the country bus;[69] but by 1960 the car was starting to make an impact on demand for bus services, reflecting the preferred qualities of private transport. Neither has car ownership in rural areas been limited to the middle classes, much car commuting being to urban employment of all kinds. A striking effect has been the shift away from Saturday bus services, once the busiest, but now less important than the rest of the week – the commuter's car is available at weekends for the family shopping trip.

The years of decline were led by the large, publicly owned companies, many of which announced that they were withdrawing from the 'deep rural' areas. Some went so far as to obtain permission to apply higher fare scales on rural services. The failure of these firms to understand marginal costs worsened the situation, but rural services even then were best left to small businesses, set in the villages and able to mix bus operation with school contracts and private hire. All the same, the main lesson to be drawn from the past thirty years is that the car has inevitably become the primary mode of rural transport, and that no gain can come from making its use more difficult and expensive. The withdrawal of Vehicle Excise Duty (perhaps in connection with electronic road pricing) would be a most effective contribution to the solution of the rural transport problem.

---

[69] I have surveyed this in *The Country Bus* (Exeter: David & Charles, 1986); further insights are to be found in *The Country Railway*, by David St John Thomas (Exeter: David & Charles, 1976).

The Weaknesses of Subsidy

The powers to subsidise bus services provided by the Transport Act 1968 were supposedly for the benefit of rural areas. In practice, the money went almost entirely to the conurbations, where it was needed least, because the concentration of demand makes for profitable bus services. As things turned out, attitudes to rural bus services came to vary widely from one shire county to another, despite the co-ordination requirements imposed by the Act (and withdrawn by the Transport Act 1985). The government's recent emergency package of Rural Bus Grants has been equally varied in its outcome, and has arguably done more harm than good. To begin with, the money was earmarked for augmenting existing services or starting new ones, and not to sustain existing ones. In a number of cases it has meant that commercially viable services have been weakened, and sometimes withdrawn, so that total sub-sidised bus mileage has increased; in many others the outcome has been buses carrying fresh air, and not a few of the services concerned were quite soon abandoned. Policies vary between authorities, but the outcome of government policy for the benefit of people living in the countryside is to say the least questionable.

Local government at county level is an urban affair, and however well-intentioned the co-ordinating officers and their staff may be, they are at more than one remove from the needs of the villages. No effective measurement of 'social need' has ever been invented, nor could it be. The limited funds are thus targeted as best may be, and there is no certainty that the twin objectives of effective delivery and allocative efficiency are achieved.

There is no way in which public transport can be provided in rural areas on the scale or frequency that has been shown to attract demand in the cities. Residents in the country should not feel guilty when they use their cars to go shopping in the local market town, or to get to the railway station. The car, together with the taxi (often shared) has become the at-need form of transport where demand is scattered and interconnection impractical. The cost of subsidising rural transport to urban standards is manifestly unthinkable.

But the country bus still has its necessary contribution to make, and some of the larger companies have made a success by improving their services where the demand can be found. Frequent, well-marketed services between towns have been successful in gaining traffic and serving villages along or near the route. By extending the service through to a housing estate on the far side of the town they can offer a local bus service that might not be justified on its own. The fact that there are areas in which far less imagination than this has been shown should not blind us to the potential of the bus in this part of the market.

Thus the traditional country bus remains important. An operator based in 'deep rural' territory can pick up passengers on a roundabout route and offer access to one or two local towns, and people in the business have shown for many years an understanding of marginal costs that would have shamed the big firms in the industry. Factory and school contracts running morning and evening offer the chance to run a local market-day service for which the driver's wages are irrelevant. And a coach operator may well attract business from local organisations through being seen to run such services, contributing to local needs.

Other potential contributors exist. There has been some success with community bus services, but they depend upon the availability of people who are willing to spare the time, and, except for the small minibus, to undertake training. The Association of Co-ordinating Officers (ATCO) has suggested that charities should be invited to sponsor services. But the suggestion that school buses should be open for public use comes up against unfortunate experiences with children's behaviour, a serious enough problem in itself.

The present system of subsidy does not fit at all well to the situation, and may often weaken its fragile economy. Local people know better than officials in far-away towns where they want to go to. But there will always remain gaps, and a residual need for subsidy. What matters is that it should be carefully targeted, and the experience of the present government's Rural Bus Grants has shown that county and district councils are not very good at that. Indeed, it is plain that in some cases they fancy themselves as network bus operators in their own right.

A much neglected solution to many of the problems of rural administration is to push decision-making down to the people immediately concerned.

> a solution . . . might be to delegate planning powers down to . . . parish level and – the very essence of the proposal – let the parish strike its own deals.[70]

If a parish council (or a group of parishes too small for each of them to have a council) were to be able to levy a rate for the purpose, the money raised could be used to 'buy in' additional services or timings, from bus or coach or taxi firms holding the necessary quality licence.[71] Alternatively, district councils (nearer to the ground than the counties) could bring together representatives of the parishes and local coach and bus firms, so that the operators could find what was being asked for, and also explain in some cases why it would be difficult to provide. In 1968 I was present at such a meeting in North Devon, and people from both sides said how useful it had been, and asked why it had never been done before. I often wonder how far it has ever been done, anywhere, since then.

Today, though, 'access to the countryside' has become an emotive political issue, and the provision of rural transport is linked for much of the year with the requirements of tourism. Although the tourist trade brings some benefits to centres of attraction, neither residents nor visitors can be happy when the situation is reached where 'the Lake

---

[70] *The Green Quadratic*, London: Adam Smith Institute, 1998, p. 24. Sadly, the present government is proposing to do away with parish councils, which shows how far policies are city-driven in this country today.

[71] There is a problem here, in that the current regulations do not make it easy for a taxi firm to operate anything like a bus service.

District is full' Many local authorities subsidise bus services for tourists, sometimes daily through the season, and sometimes on Sundays only, and these can be useful for residents as well; we must hope that there is some attempt at market pricing. But the congestion problem is a very serious matter, involving external costs that are not passed on to the motorist, and it must be plain that some form of road-use pricing would help ease the problem, not least by reducing bus operators' costs accordingly, and enabling them to offer improved levels of service. It is worth remembering that buses and coaches are remarkably efficient in that one coach carries as many people as 20 cars.

Summing Up

Public transport can never be an effective substitute for the private car where population density is low. To provide the frequency that customers demand is impracticable, other than on the busy inter-urban routes. But with the car or the taxi as the prime provider, buses and coaches still have an important part to play. The provision of rural bus services, including school transport, has a delicate balance, and for local government administrators to intervene with subsidy, however well-intentioned, can only too easily disturb it. To the extent that support is needed, decisions should be taken at the level of government closest to the area that is to be served. People who choose to live away from the urban environment do in general accept that they cannot expect the same level of public transport.

VIII. The Movement of Goods

Road and Rail

There seems to be a commonly held belief that the development of the steam railway put an end to road transport. This is far from the truth,[72] and indeed the movement of goods by road was vital to the economy throughout the Railway Age. But it was not until the later 1920s that the railways started to feel the impact of the commercial motor vehicle, as new and improved roads and more reliable lorries made their impact. At first largely used for delivery services, from the 1930s the diesel engine made longer journeys practicable, and Barker and Gerhold comment that hauliers 'concentrated upon particular traffics over medium distances while the railways, obliged as common carriers to accept any goods offered to them, were left with the rest'.[73]

Licensing came into effect under the Road and Rail Traffic Act 1933, which introduced quality control, and required hauliers to hold one of three types of licence: the 'A' licence, for general carriage of customers' goods; the 'C' licence, for the carriage of the licensee's own goods only; and the 'B' licence, which added to this the right to carry other's goods within certain limits. No attempt at price control was made, and the railway companies continued to be at the disadvantage of being common carriers, having to publish their rates; hauliers could inspect these, and then undercut them.

The period of nationalisation that followed the Transport Act 1947 saw little meaningful integration of road and rail

---

[72] See Theo Barker and Dorian Gerhold, *The Rise and Rise of Road Transport*, 1700–1990, London: Macmillan, 1993.

[73] *Op cit*, p. 63.

transport. Under the British Transport Commission the Road Haulage Executive and the Railway Executive remained separate trading entities, and there was a 'Chinese wall' dividing them. Indeed, the road haulage managers continued to seek traffic where they could find it, much of it coming from the railway, which, still a common carrier, was in the same position as it had been in the 1930s. Furthermore, the 'C licence' firms had been exempted from compulsory purchase, and many companies expanded their fleets, through dissatisfaction with state-owned services or even as a matter of principle.[74]

Denationalisation was a slow and complex process, completed in 1980 with the sale of the National Freight Corporation to its managers and staff; deregulation had been achieved by the Labour government's Transport Act of 1968; while the railways had been freed from common carrier status and the need to publish their routes as early as 1962. But just as car ownership grew exponentially after 1950, so also did road transport develop on a scale that had equally been unforeseen. Table 6 sets out the shift from rail to road over the years; a change that was influenced strongly by the shift of the national economy away from heavy industry. Road goods transport today is a mix of heavy haulage and of what is now called distribution.

The truly revolutionary change over the past forty years has been the growth of national and international provision for the distribution of commodities of all kinds, with the development of sophisticated supply-chain management. This has made possible the spread of supermarkets, and also the decay of small businesses that once contributed to the resources and welfare of local communities and suburban high streets. It has been entirely dependent on the construction of the motorway system, which indeed was intended to provide for a 'modern transport system' (and not for the private motorist, whose growing demand was hardly foreseen in the 1950s, when the government committed itself to motorways). But the next step, following

---

[74] The subject is extremely well covered by Bonavia 1987. *Op. cit.*

Table 6 Trends in Domestic Freight Transport, 1975-1998

Goods moved (billion tonne kilometres)

Year	Road	Rail	Water	Pipeline	All modes
1975	92	21	28	6	147
1980	93	18	54	10	175
1985	103	15	58	11	187
1990	136	16	56	11	219
1995	150	13	53	11	227
1996	154	15	55	12	236
1997	157	17	48	11	233
1998	160	17	57[a]	11[a]	246[a]

Goods lifted (million tonnes)

Year	Road	Rail	Water	Pipeline	All modes
1975	1,514	175	108	52	1,846
1980	1,395	154	137	83	1,769
1985	1,452	122	142	89	1,805
1990	1,749	140	152	121	2,162
1995	1,701	101	143	168	2,113
1996	1,730	102	142	157	2,131
1997	1,740	105	142	148	2,135
1998	1,727	101	149[a]	148[a]	2,126[a]

[a] Provisional figures. 'Water' includes all UK coastwise and one-port freight movements by sea, and inland waterway traffic. ('One-port' movements are typically servicing oil rigs).

Source: *Transport Statistics Great Britain 1999 Edition*, Government Statistical Service.

After a steady fall during the last years of state ownership, rail freight is starting to hold its own. Note the varying volume of pipeline traffic; pipelines are in competition with rail but not with road.

from the growth of e-commerce, seems likely to bring new problems, as residential streets become crowded with delivery vehicles. (Some e-commerce firms have failed to log on to the logistics of their business, with consequent delays and customer dissatisfaction.)

Railways are well suited for the carriage of large loads over medium to long distances, or on a frequent, regular basis over shorter ones. But for distribution they require too much trans-shipment, with the risks of damage and pilferage that involves, along with road congestion at terminals. Only the truck can offer the advantages of 'serving all sites', and today's night-time movement of road-borne goods through the distribution hubs of the midlands is part of a highly efficient, competitive industry, linked into international road, sea and air movement; much of it offering guaranteed overnight delivery. Alongside this there is the carriage of more traditional cargoes, like steel and building materials, and the retail trade has its own network of delivery to shops and supermarkets. And the industry functions with no direct subsidy – indeed, it is reasonable to argue that it is over-taxed.

Vehicle Excise Duty (VED) and fuel tax are being used by the government as sumptuary taxation, but the 'fuel tax escalator' introduced by the last Conservative government had a disastrous effect upon the efficiency of the industry, far from acting as a 'green' constraint on mileage. It is to be hoped that the Chancellor's recent adjustment of the process will bring some relief to a hard-pressed industry, where diesel prices increased by 20% in 1999 (partly because of higher crude oil prices). One result has been a major disadvantage for UK companies competing with operators from the continent and the Republic of Ireland, since the introduction of cabotage has allowed them to carry loads entirely within the UK, with a base in Britain but often using cheaper fuel from across the Channel. Some UK firms have already 'out-flagged' part of their fleets to bases on the continent. VED and fuel tax could be reduced as part of a bargain for electronic pricing for the use of motorways and main highways, which in itself would be far more beneficial in leading to allocative efficiency.

The industry is made up of a limited number of large firms, often trading through subsidiary companies, and a very much larger number of small ones, many of them one-man businesses working as subcontractors. Competition is intense, and freight rates today are roughly at the level at which they were ten years ago. The problem of the 'back-load', where marginal cost is virtually zero, creating a temptation to cut prices so as to maintain cash flow, which bedevilled the industry in the 1930s, is starting to reappear. It seems certain that there are more firms in the market than it can stand, but any necessary shakeout is impossible so long as the problem of the escalator remains. Government should certainly do something to help the haulage and distribution sectors.

Some Alternatives

The unpopularity of road goods transport among the chattering classes and in the anti-road lobbies is absurd and ignorant. Sheer bad planning has played a great part in causing much of the congestion that exists; it is stupid for the M20 and part of the M42 to have been built as four-lane roads, and the release of land for housing along the M25, which was not allowed for in its planning, flooded it with car commuting – for which, as we have seen, motorways were never intended. New motorway and by-pass construction is urgently needed at various 'pinch points', of which the Birmingham Northern Relief Road is a classic example. An effective and efficient road transport system should not be put at risk by the politically correct.

But there are other alternatives, each in its way constructive and tending to allocative efficiency. As we have seen in Chapter 5, one of the success stories of railway privatisation has been the growth of freight transport, neglected so long by British Rail. The strategic rail link through the English midlands to connect with the Channel Tunnel will take time to complete, and although Table 7 shows that rail-linked 'distribution parks' are still relatively few in number, they are now becoming established. While the ignorant response to congestion – 'send it all by train' – fails to recognise that the greater part of freight will continue to move by road because that is more efficient, yet the railway can still ease the problem – to the advantage of the freight operators themselves. Even so, there is reason to believe that too much surplus railway land is still being sold by the British Railways Board, which could be used for the development of rail-connected terminals.

The cry is still to be heard: 'Why don't we make more use of the canals?' To this the immediate answer is simple: the British canal system could never compete with the railway in its day, and the narrow waterways are quite irrelevant to the needs of industry at present, though they form the basis of much recreational cruising. There is, in fact, little or no future for canal traffic between two points within this country. The significant waterways today are those like the tidal Thames, the Manchester Ship Canal, the Humber and the Yorkshire Ouse, the lower Trent, and some of the waterways in East Anglia, where freight movement is international in character. Inland waterways in Britain have tended to suffer from the activities of the sentimental

Table 7 Distribution Parks with Rail-linked Access, 1999

Region	On-site (active)	On-site (planned)	Close by	Further away	Possible	Total number of parks
South-east	–	1	2	2	2	84
South-west	1	4	1	1	1	49
Midlands	2	4	–	–	–	101
North-west	1	3	5	–	–	73
North-east and Scotland	1	1	3	1	–	44
Total	5	12	11	4	3	351

The columns show those parks with actual or planned rail-linked access

Source: *Distribution Business*, Guide to UK Distribution Parks, 1999.

enthusiast, but through the efforts of the late Charles Hadfield an Inland Shipping Group exists,[75] which has produced a blueprint for development of those that have a promising future, including both road and rail tranship-ment facilities. It is sad to record that the promising operation of BACAT (Barge Aboard CATamaran) shipping, to link the Rhine waterways with the Humber ports, introduced in 1974, was withdrawn after a few months following industrial action by Hull dockers.

Waterways suitable for seagoing vessels form part of the coastwise trade that played a small but significant part in the movement of goods until in 1947 the Dock Workers (Regulation of Employment) Act sent it into 'terminal decline'.[76] Since the repeal of the Act there has already been a return of trade to the waters around our coasts.[77] Previously limited to oil, roadstone, shrinking quantities of power-station coal, and some china clay, coasters are now starting to move goods that previously went by road. Cargo, including containers, can be as readily moved in this way as by the ships that cross the narrow seas. To the extent that state support is justified, improving port facilities and access to them, to reverse the trends that originated from deeply mistaken policies, it rests on economic efficiency and reduced pollution,[78] and Mr Prescott is known to be aware of it. Early this year (2000) the Shipping Minister

---

[75] See Joseph Boughey, *Charles Hadfield – Canal Man and More* (Strood, Sutton Publishing, 1998), esp. pp. 97–102. *UK Freight Waterways: A Blueprint for the Future* (1996) is available from the Inland Waterways Association.

[76] The words are taken from a paper by Joe Rayner, Raising the portcullis: repeal of the National Dock Labour Scheme and the employment relationship in the docks industry, *Economic Affairs*, 19(2), June 1999, p. 7.

[77] *Waterborne Freight in the United Kingdom 1998* (London, DETR, 1999) reports that 'the . . . total tonnage of domestic waterborne freight transport in 1998 was 7.6 million tonnes (5%) higher at 149.4 million tonnes, largely reflecting an increase in coastwise traffic'.

[78] See Michael Everard, Coastal and short-sea shipping: an alternative to roads, *Proceedings of the Chartered Institute of Transport*, 4(4), 1995, pp. 3–10.

announced plans to modernise the Trust Ports (those that remained in public ownership after the nationalised ports were privatised).

Summing Up

It must be accepted that promising opportunities exist for the movement of goods by road to be reduced, chiefly by a shift to rail, but to some extent also to water, although the consequences will not be substantial. The key to the future must lie in a balanced policy of road-use pricing and new construction, including recognition that the motorways are economically more significant for freight movement than for the private car. And surely it is here that the true meaning of 'integration' becomes clear, bringing the provision and pricing of road and rail track under the same regime.

IX. Some Conclusions

An Industry of Low Repute

The twentieth century has seen the growth of urbanisation throughout the world. In the United Kingdom today the development of physical distribution has produced what is very largely an urban society. But at the heart of the matter the fundamental things remain: civilisation, which by definition is life in cities, is entirely dependent on three industries; *agriculture, public health* and *transport*. And these rank lowest in social approval, attracting interest only when things go wrong. Take a representative icon for each in turn: the farm labourer, the dustman, the truck driver: how many careers advisers would recommend these industries to the school-leaver?

There is no space here to reflect upon the market failures of agriculture, nor the problems of historic cost accounting that beset the authorities responsible for sewage. The rescue services – police, fire and ambulance (though rarely coastguard) – figure on television constantly, whereas transport *operation* seldom figures even in the soap operas.[79] Perhaps it is only right that we should expect the industry to be so effective as never to attract public interest – which, indeed, only comes into play when things go wrong. What is perhaps even more interesting is the extent to which logistics and tourism, which depend upon transport for their livelihood, treat it with the same lack of interest. It is an industry of low repute. But there is a price to pay, in the ignorance of the public and the media, and in the low reputation of the transport industry among educators and

---

[79] Some years ago there was a television series called *The Brothers*, which was based on a family road transport firm, but it told the viewer very little about the management of a busy haulage business.

politicians. The post of Minister of Transport has tended, since it was invented in 1919, to be held by politicians at the start or towards the end of their careers. Barbara Castle's very success in the post led to her being seen as a threat to Harold Wilson. Very few ministers have held the office for long, and the Department does not rank high in the world of the Civil Service.[80] The general ignorance is illustrated all too well by the examples given in Box 5.

Box 5 A Bad Image

Two recent examples illustrate what the transport industry has to put up with, in ignorant or mistaken comment through the media. First, a hatchet job on the part of the BBC. This was an attack in the programme *Top Gear* in November 1999, making sweeping and completely false statements about the commendable Oxford Bus Strategy, which, among other things, has seen an increase of 65% in bus use over the past decade. The BBC was inundated with complaints, from, among others, Oxfordshire County Council and the Oxford Bus Company, a Go Ahead subsidiary, and was forced to admit that the programme did not meet the expected standards of fairness, accuracy and due impartiality .An opportunity , it said, would be taken to 'cover/ the topic in a more balanced way' – but by now the damage will have been done. Even less forgivable was the clanger dropped by the RAC in its annual *Report on Motoring* in 2000, where it was claimed that commuting by public transport takes three times longer than by private car. In its response the Confederation of Passenger Transport pointed out that 'for most people in London, going to work by car takes longer, and elsewhere, it is unlikely that the average public transport journey would take three times longer'. This was repeated in the national media, and it is impossible to follow up and correct errors like this. Many other statements in the report were open to criticism, and the interesting conclusion was that motorists tend not to know what their own costs are, and have no idea of the equivalent price by public transport, or even what the alternatives are. Buses, trains and cars compete In the market for people movement, but it is important that the consumer in the market has accurate and unbiased information.

---

[80] Be it said, though, that there have been some outstanding permanent secretaries, and a number of departmental officials have shown a serious interest in the transport industry, and the need to introduce market disciplines.

A Suitable Case for Markets

Despite the increasing evidence of the success of deregulation and privatisation over the past twenty years (and more, where road freight transport is concerned) there remains a widely held opinion (for that is all that it is) that the transport industry should be subject to centralised control by a public authority. That there is not a shred of evidence that this would work suggests that the novelist Colin Macinnes was right to suggest that 'England is . . . a country infested with people who love to tell us what to do, but who very rarely seem to know what's going on'.[81] What is generally forgotten by such people is that it was tried once, when the British Transport Commission (BTC) was set up in 1947, and that the experience of the BTC showed that centralised planning would not work. What is more, with today's understanding of non-linear relationships[82] we know that it never could work.

Both theory and experience make it plain that the market must be the preferred solution to the 'transport problem'. Set the market free, so far as it is possible to do so, and there will be a growing tendency towards greater effectiveness, as firms seek out and satisfy real demand, and greater efficiency in the allocation of scarce resources. To the economist this is obvious, but it appears that in the present state of public knowledge it is but little understood. From the days of Nicholas Ridley to those of John Prescott there has been a steady drift towards *dirigisme*, and it looks set to become a torrent. In a recent bulletin we may read

> Alas, in the eighties, integration became a dirty word and the dream was never fulfilled. Now integration is 'in' again. . . .[83]

---

[81] Quoted in Matthew Parris (ed.), *Scorn, with Added Vitriol*, London: Hamish Hamilton, 2nd edn., 1995, p. 87.

[82] See David Parker and Ralph Stacey, *Chaos, Management and Economics: the implications of non-linear thinking*, London: IEA, Hobart Paper 125, 1994.

[83] Transport Studies Society, *Newsletter 182*, September 1999.

That is integration from above, to be directed by those who claim to know better than the users of transport what is good for the industry and its customers. The Strategic Rail Authority and the provisions for bus franchising in the Transport Bill are its messengers. The anti-car lobby is with them in seeking forcibly to constrain freedom of choice, while the nihilist attitude to road construction and improvement,[84] common throughout politics, might be designed to maintain the present allocative distortion. Yet since top-down integration is unworkable, how are we to achieve an efficient framework for the transport industries?

Integration, Market-led

If integration has any meaning today it is the urgent need for rational pricing of the transport infrastructure. Neither is this new: railway and road transport interests have argued for half a century that each is unfairly treated. If ever the term 'a level playing-field' were justified, it is appropriate here. Without it, the market cannot function in the way Ponsonby visualised it;[85] without it, every intervention designed to improve effectiveness is bound to fail; indeed, it is more than likely to make things worse. Professor Newbery's argument[86] for a company responsible for the provision, maintenance and new construction of both road and rail track offers the basic requirement for a functioning transport market.

Much thought would be needed about the pricing policy, but the objective is plain: to attract traffic to that part of the infrastructure that has the lowest congestion factor. The logistics of freight transport are such that a pricing system of this kind would lead to the transfer of goods from road to rail without any of the distortions inevitable from intervention. Steps would be needed to obviate delays associated

---

[84] See Sir Christopher Foster, The dangers of nihilism in roads policy, *Proceedings of the Chartered Institute of Transport*, 4(2), 1995, pp. 22–45.

[85] Ponsonby 1969, *op. cit.*

[86] See p. 7.

with planning procedures, as the highways ceased to be a government responsibility, and public opinion would need to be addressed so as to explain the futility of opposition to needed new construction (road or rail) by Messrs NIMBY and Swampy.[87] Nevertheless, this is but the start.

In the background there is the problem of taxation, and the resentment of motorists and commercial operators at the amount taken from them in the form of fuel tax and Vehicle Excise Duty (VED). Since an integrated track authority or company would use electronic road-use pricing, there would be the inevitable protest that 'we pay enough to use the roads already'. No progress is likely unless the issues here are made plain, and an improvement achieved in the state of public knowledge.

Road vehicles, however owned, are of course subject to sumptuary taxation. This is nothing new: private carriages were taxed from an early date, and in 1775 a duty of one halfpenny per mile was imposed on the stage coaches. There is no difference in principle between taxes on travel, and the taxation of alcohol and tobacco – or, in their day, the window tax and the tea duty. Where demand is highly inelastic, governments will impose taxes (and 'escalate' them), and it would be surprising if they did not. Commodity taxes, such as those on tea, coffee, sugar and other things, have been swept away, and indeed would be unthinkable today, but whereas tobacco and alcohol may be seen as luxuries, transport is without doubt a necessity; arguments by the anti-car lobby notwithstanding. So the taxation issue is one that must be faced, if integration is to succeed.

And this is where the government's policies are at their weakest, for it is here that there is least freedom of action. Abolish fuel duty and VED for buses and coaches and the industry stands ready to improve services and encourage less use of cars. Abolish VED for cars, as a partial *quid pro quo*

---

[87] NIMBY: acronym for 'not in my back yard'. Swampy: a code name for an objector who 'digs in' to prevent needed investment from being achieved.

for urban road-use pricing, and the rural transport problem will be greatly eased. Abolish VED and reduce fuel duty for commercial road freight transport as a *quid pro quo* for interurban road pricing and you remove an unjustified burden on hauliers, which currently puts them at a disadvantage in competition with firms from the European continent who can trade freely over here. Abolition of the fuel tax would best be considered as part of a wider reform of highway pricing policy. There are arguments for and against each such policy, but whether any would be acceptable to HM Treasury is another matter.

None the less, there are times when it is necessary to be radical or to lose out. Public opinion ranks transport pretty low, and displays little interest in policy, unless it would affect the motorist. The idea of an integrated policy at track level – a market for the use of roads and rails – needs to be explained and justified, in terms of the efficient use of scarce resources. Recognising that the internet, ports and some waterways, are also 'track providers' shows how demand for movement for various purposes can find its own preferred satisfaction, leading to greater effectiveness. And it is from there that a competitive market in movement, of goods and passengers and information, can be relied upon to develop fairly, leading to the 'integration' that Mr Prescott seeks, as well as to the 'co-ordination' that has been pursued for so long, with so little attempt to define the term.

Against *Dirigisme*

Integration from the top down – trusting the 'platonic guardians' – implies that public transport is 'not a commercial service like all the others', which is the view of M Jean-Paul Bailly, the President of the International Union of Public Transport (UITP).[88]

One weakness of this argument is the presumed distinction between 'public transport' (assumed to be for

---

[88] See p. 13.

passengers) and 'private transport', which must mean the private car. So far, policy debate has too often taken this for granted, as if the car were not 'just another form of transport'. Integration as proposed here, literally 'from the ground up', brings all modes together, and by bringing marginal costs to the attention of car users goes some way to 'commercialising' that part of the industry too. The weaknesses in present policy and the state of the various modes that we have examined here are invariably related to the mistaken interventions of successive governments, whether in the regulatory policies or by fiscal means. Transport – whether public or private – is too important to be left to the politicians.

Yet some intervention is required. Transport is a 'fail-dangerous' industry, and its technology is opaque,[89] which means that safety standards need to be supervised. The market is imperfect, especially for bus and train services, where the sunk costs of the established firms offset the potential of contestability, and the consequent pressure to combine has to be constrained. Sumptuary taxation is going to remain, even if the public can be made to see it for what it is. On the other hand, the powers of land-use and regional planners and the ever-present threat of the NIMBY persuasion require intervention to give greater freedom to the market for new construction of track and ease of access for vehicles. The emotional and often irrational attitudes of both motorists and anti-car protesters must be faced with reality, and a clear political line – preferably cross-party – should be taken. The car, after all, is today what the bus once was seen to be: the *people's chariot*.

These are some of the requirements for policy. But unless it is generally accepted that transport is not *'something different'*, but just another industry best left alone to serve

---

[89] The best-qualified engineer, leave alone the layman, cannot assess the safety of the vehicle or vessel to which she is invited to entrust herself or her goods, nor the capability of its 'driver' or the technical or managerial efficiency of the firm.

the public, confusion will continue to reign, and integration, however defined, will never be achieved.

Effectiveness, which is what people want, is the predictable outcome of competitive efficiency. There are too many barriers and distortions in the market for movement today, perhaps the greatest of them arising from the tendency of every government to meddle. The present government's policies, confused and confusing as they are, promise to carry the art of meddling to new heights, and the mirage of future franchise is perhaps the most dangerous of them. But to introduce policies leading to greater efficiency must take time, and the concept of allocative efficiency is not an easy one to introduce to the public as an explanation for delays in the development of more effective provision of transport. Attitudes in much of the European Union, including Ireland, tend to favour dirigisme (and this may even be true in Scotland).

The problem is the extent to which public opinion within the United Kingdom finds it unacceptable to see bus and rail transport in commercial hands, and resents the successes of men like Sir Richard Branson and Brian Souter. The media reflect this, and, as we have seen (Box 5) it is not infrequent to find commentators demonstrating considerable ignorance about the state of the industry. New regulations make it difficult for road transport firms of all kinds to recruit and train staff from school-leavers. Financial interests suffer from short-termism, while the bus and coach industry and the railways need investment in both people and equipment that must take time to produce the organic growth that is there to be harvested. What is certain is this: that sensible government policies can help, but they should not be on the scale of intervention that the White Paper envisaged, and the Transport Bill promises. The whole content of policy today is to centralise power over railways, buses and the so fashionable trams, and to succumb to the environmentalist's dislike of road goods transport. This *melange* can in no way deliver effective supply or tend to allocative efficiency.

Left alone, there can be no doubt that transport will perform well in the effective provision of services. Only a tendency towards cartelisation in modes with high sunk costs, and a temptation to take short-cuts on safety, could be criticised. In terms of allocative efficiency the whole industry is constrained by the problem of external costs, some of them environmental, but the greatest problem is the distortion that follows inevitably from the irrationality of infrastructure pricing. Integration at that level is the essential step that will enable a market-led industry to continue to co-ordinate supply and demand, without the inappropriate intervention of well-meaning government administrators.

Regulation Without The State...
The Debate Continues

John Blundell
Colin Robinson

The rising tide of government regulation in most countries is provoking a reconsideration of the extent to which the state should lay down rules for others. Self-regulation and other forms of voluntary rule-setting are being examined as substitutes for regulation by government.

Readings 52 begins with a paper by John Blundell and Colin Robinson which analyses the forces behind government regulation, its shortcomings and the scope for voluntary regulation. Seven papers by distinguished commentators on regulation then examine Blundell and Robinson's conclusions.

Contents

The Institute of Economic Affairs
2 Lord North Street, Westminster, London SW1P 3LB
Telephone: 020 7799 3745 Facsimile: 020 7799 2137
E-mail: iea@iea.org.uk Internet: http://www.iea.org.uk ISBN 0-255 36483-0

£10.00